And Now
FOR SOMETHING
Completely
TRIVIAL
THE MONTY PYTHON TRIVIA
AND QUIZ BOOK

FOR GRAHAM

And Now
FOR SOMETHING
Completely
TRIVIAL

THE MONTY PYTHON TRIVIA
AND QUIZ BOOK

By Kim "Howard" Johnson

ST. MARTIN'S PRESS   NEW YORK

Monty Python's royalty from this book will again go to the Rainforest Action Network, 301 Broadway, Suite A, San Francisco, CA 94133.

Design by Judy Dannecker

Luibrary of Congress Cataloging-in-Publication Data

Johnson, Kim.
    And now for something completely trivial : the Monty Python trivia and quiz book / Kim "Howard" Johnson.
        p.   cm.
    "A Thomas Dunne book."
    ISBN 0-312-06289-3
    1. Monty Python (Comedy troupe) 2. English wit and humor.
    I. Title.
    PN6175.J64—1991
    791.45'72—dc20   91-20915
                                                                    CIP

First Edition: September 1991

10 9 8 7 6 5 4 3 2 1

Author's Note

I thought I had thrown enough Python information into my previous book, *The First 200 Years of Monty Python,* to satisfy the most fervent fans of the group.

Apparently, I was wrong.

It seems that Monty Python followers are a fanatical lot, eagerly devouring everything they can find related to the group. They are interested in the smallest minutia about the TV shows and films and take a fierce, perverse pride in their knowledge of all things Python.

This, then, is the book for them.

Within these pages are listed all the appearances of the Colonel and the Knight with the rubber chicken; quizzes ranging from the laughably easy to the brain-hurting difficult; and curious bits of information guaranteed to be utterly useless to anyone.

But this is also a book for the more casual Python observer.

Included are the first appearances of the Gumbys and the Pantomime Goose; the book lists the characters and objects crushed by the sixteen-ton weight; and it details *all* the Arthurs and Kens in the TV shows.

How could any devoted fan—or mildly curious viewer—ask for more?

SPECIAL THANKS DEPARTMENT: A book like this would obviously be impossible without the advice, assistance, and encouragement of so many people that I would certainly leave someone out if I tried to mention them all. However, I couldn't possibly *not* thank my agent, Dominick Abel; my parents; Anne James and all at Mayday Management; George Harrison; and of course the Pythons themselves.

Show by Any Other Name . . .

When the group first got together to do a show for the BBC, they eventually had to come up with a title for their new series. A number of titles were rejected for various reasons before they finally decided on *Monty Python's Flying Circus,* including those listed below.

■ *The Circus*—This was the original name used by BBC executives to refer to the show even before the group members themselves were involved. It was BBC producer Barry Took that conceived the idea of hiring young writers and performers to create a comedy/variety show of their own.
■ *The Flying Circus*—The original title evolved into this, so that the BBC would have some method of referring to it in their internal memos.
■ *Baron von Took's Flying Circus*—This was another BBC invention, which indicates just how closely Barry Took was involved in the eyes of his co-workers. Again, it was never referred to as this outside the BBC.

When the group members became directly involved, they started coming up with titles of their own, but they couldn't choose one they were happy with. As Michael Palin puts it, "They worked one afternoon, and the next morning people weren't quite so sure."

■ *It* and *It's*—These were apparently the first titles suggested by the group members themselves, although the BBC was less than enthusiastic. Michael Palin feels these titles may have been responsible in part for the "It's" Man.

■ *Bunn, Wackett, Buzzard, Stubble, and Boot, The Toad Elevating Moment,* and *A Horse, a Spoon, and a Basin*—These were among the titles discarded and never used by the Pythons, although John Cleese was particularly fond of the first of these—it was actually written into some of the rehearsal scripts but was never used for anything other than trivia books.

■ *Owl Stretching Time, Whither Canada?,* and *Sex and Violence*—These discarded titles all ended up as titles of individual shows and were used either at the beginning or end of shows in the first series. The latter was their response when the BBC told them, "We hope there isn't any sex and violence (in the show)."

The Pythons' continuing indecision led the BBC to become somewhat impatient, according to Barry Took; at one point, the group actually threatened to call the show by a different title each week. "The BBC finally told them, 'It doesn't matter what you call it as long as the words *flying circus* are in it,' because all the notes and memos going around internally at the BBC called it 'The Circus.' It would confuse the BBC if they called it anything else, so they went away and invented Monty Python."

Actually, it wasn't quite that simple.

■ *Gwen Dibley's Flying Circus*—This was a favorite of Michael Palin's. He picked up Dibley's name in one of his mother's newspapers and thought it would be a nice surprise for this woman—whoever she was—to discover that she'd had a new BBC show named for her. One apocryphal story has it that Dibley was Michael's piano teacher when he was eleven years old, but he claims it was a name he picked out of a newspaper account of a women's institute meeting. At any rate, this was another suggestion that somehow didn't seem as funny the next morning, and because of that—and the possibility of a law-suit—Dibley lost her chance at immortality.

■ *Monty Python's Flying Circus*—At last, a winner. As things were getting down to the wire and they *had* to choose a title, this seemed like the one that no one really disliked (although they weren't as keen on it the next morning, either).

Many longtime fans are familiar with the story of how they decided upon the final name: They tried to think of the kind of person who would be likely to present the sort of show they wanted to do. They felt that a Python was a very slithery sort of creature, while Monty sounded like the kind of unscrupulous entrepreneur that would fit together well with Python—John Cleese reportedly contributed the latter, while Eric Idle was apparently responsible for the former. And the name was written on the BBC notes and memos, ensuring its permanence.

Confuse-a-Cat, Ltd., Recruitment Test

Applicants wishing to work for as prestigious a company as Confuse-a-Cat, Ltd., must face rigorous testing to determine their feline acumen and their ability to look into the mind of *Felis domesticus* to ascertain the necessary stimulus.

In other words, one must be aware of what will shake a cat out of its complacency. Below are listed a number of persons or things used to confuse cats, along with a few extraneous items. Which three items do *not* belong in the Confuse-a-Cat program?

Long John Silver	Julius Caesar
Napoléon	raw chicken
Mr. Gumby	Nude man
cannon	Two chefs
Sixteen-ton weight	Boxers
Traffic policeman	Penguin on a pogo stick

**or the First Time**

Initial Appearances of Recurring Favorites

Throughout the forty-five *Monty Python's Flying Circus* TV shows, a number of favorite characters and bits occurred several times. Characters like the "It's" Man were part of Python lore from the very first show, but others, such as the Gumbys and the Nude Organist, came along later. Below are the very first appearances of some Python favorites, in order of their introduction to viewers.

THE PEPPERPOTS

The initial appearance of the appalling older ladies—whom Graham Chapman always referred to as Pepperpots—was, not surprisingly, in the very first show recorded. Played by John Cleese, Terry Jones, Graham Chapman, and Michael Palin, they responded to an offscreen interviewer who asked them about the French, and they also spoke admiringly of French philosophers.

"AND NOW FOR SOMETHING COMPLETELY DIFFERENT"

The classic Python catchphrase was also used in the very first show recorded (although it was the second one broadcast), but it was not spoken by John Cleese, who eventually came to be associated with it more than any of the others.

The first Python to say, "And now for something completely different," was actually Eric Idle, playing an announcer at a desk who introduces "a man with three buttocks."

WOMEN'S INSTITUTE APPLAUSE

The brief film clip of an audience of old ladies applauding (Michael Palin says it looks quite a bit like the audiences at their initial taping) came to be associated with Python, although the footage was used less often in subsequent seasons. Initially discovered by one of the show's researchers, Sarah Hart Dyke, the ladies also appeared in the first show ever recorded. They made their first appearance applauding a man with two noses.

CAROL CLEVELAND

The First Lady, the seventh Python, was part of it all from the very first show. Her first on-camera appearance was as Mrs. Arthur (Deidre) Putey in the Marriage Guidance Counselor Sketch, falling in love with the Counselor while her husband stammers their story. And, her long association with Python was under way.

THE KNIGHT (WITH THE RUBBER CHICKEN)

The Knight, usually played by Terry Gilliam, generally walked incongruously into a scene, hit someone with a rubber chicken, and then left. His first appearance was also in the Marriage Guidance Counselor Sketch, walking in at the end to hit Arthur Putey.

VOX POPS

The Vox Pops (voice of the people) segments were utilized regularly by the Pythons. The one-liners, often shot while the group was on location doing the series' film segments, were the perfect opportunity for quick jokes and experimentation with strange new characters and were usually about one general topic. The first such segment, from the first show filmed, featured the "public" giving its views on the Mouse Problem.

FIRST HISTORICAL CHARACTER

The first appearance of a real-life character from history was in the first show aired (actually the second one filmed). The show began with a program called "It's Wolfgang Amadeus Mozart" and featured John Cleese in the title role as host, presenting historical deaths.

THE COLONEL

One of the best-loved of all Python characters, Graham Chapman's Colonel makes his first appearance in the first show aired, acting in the Joke Warfare Sketch. Most of the Colonel's subsequent appearances, however, are much briefer and more incongruous, often walking into a sketch and stopping it for being too silly. This more typical role began in Show #4 Owl Stretching Time, when he appeared through the program berating people for using variations of the army slogan "It's a Man's Life in the Modern Army."

TERRY GILLIAM

The Python animator was reluctant to appear before the camera in the early days of the Flying Circus, although he was acting fairly often by the fourth series. His first appearances usually saw him heavily costumed, as in the Knight's armor, but his first role in which he is clearly visible was also in the Joke Warfare Sketch; he plays a Nazi guard who falls victim to the Killer Joke.

THE SIXTEEN-TON WEIGHT

The huge sixteen-ton weight that would fall from the ceiling onto various people was like an element of Terry Gilliam's animation come to life. It was used periodically throughout the shows, but its first use was during the Self-defense Against Fresh Fruit Sketch; the Royal Sergeant Major drops it on a recruit attacking him with a raspberry.

THE GUMBYS

Mr. Gumby made his first appearance in the fifth show ("Man's Crisis of Identity in the Latter Half of the Twentieth Century"), although he was never identified by name and only made a brief appearance in a Vox Pop. He actually came about when the group was shooting some film segments on location. He put together the costume to deliver an opinion about customs regulations.

Although that was the first time a Gumby appeared on camera, Michael Palin says Cleese actually put the costume together to deliver the line "I'd tax people who stand in water" while (naturally) standing in a stream. It appears this was the first Gumby line filmed, although the speech on customs regulations was aired first.

It was several shows later (in "The Ant, an Introduction") that the character was identified by name. Shortly after "The Lumberjack Song," Graham Chapman, in full costume and identified by a caption as Prof. R. J. Gumby, hits himself in the head with bricks while singing "Only Make-believe." All but Gilliam would go on to portray the Gumbys quite regularly throughout the series.

MR. PRALINE

Although less distinctive than many of his other characters, John Cleese enjoyed portraying the peculiar Mr. Praline, who was often paired with Eric Idle's Mr. Badger. Praline—best known as the man who tries to return a dead parrot—makes his first appearance in the first series as a policeman, questioning the proprietor of the Whizzo Chocolate Company (in "The BBC Entry for the Zinc Stoat of Budapest").

THE VERCOTTI BROTHERS

Dino and Luigi Vercotti (played by Terry Jones and Michael Palin), the two Sicilian "businessmen," popped up individually and together in various places, usually under suspicious circumstances. Their first sketch in the first series (in "Full Frontal Nudity") showed them less subtle than usual, as they try to sell the Colonel insurance for his army in the Army Protection Racket Sketch.

INSPECTOR HARRY "SNAPPER" ORGANS

The intrepid policeman makes his initial appearance in the final show of the first series. His middle initial and his division changed throughout the remaining shows. In this first appearance, he is played by Michael Palin, although Terry Jones takes over the part in all his later sketches. He makes his Python debut briefly discussing the role of magic by the police force.

THE NUDE ORGANIST

The man playing the organ fanfare—while in the nude—first appeared, very briefly, in Show #18 (series 2, show 5). During the Blackmail Sketch, host Wally Wiggins is occasionally interrupted by the nude man playing chords on the organ.

Interestingly, the nude man in the fright wig, who has come to be associated with Terry Jones, is portrayed by Terry Gilliam in his first two appearances (here, and later in the Crackpot Religions Sketch, in which the organ fanfare accompanies the night's star prize, the Norwich City Council), both in the second series. Since nearly all the shows in the third series revealed a nude Terry Jones playing the organ fanfare just before the opening titles, Gilliam's initial two appearances in the role make him the forgotten nude man.

THE PANTOMIME GOOSE

The Pantomime Goose, along with other pantomimic creatures, would enjoy several brief appearances in the later Python shows. It is first seen, very briefly, as part of the orgy crowd in "Ken Russell's 'Gardening Club (1958)'" Show #29 (series 3, show 3).

GIANT HAMMER

Another Gilliam animation come to life, this extra-large prop first appears in Show #30. Terry Jones, as Mrs. Scab, unscrambles letters to spell "Merchant Bank" and receives the hammer on the head as her reward.

NEIL INNES

Although many Python fans have come to associate Neil Innes quite closely with the group, it may be surprising to some to discover that he did not appear on the TV show until the final series (on "Anything Goes/The Light Entertainment War"). His first major appearance was as a World War II airman, singing "When Does a Dream Begin?" to a WAAF on grainy black-and-white film.

His association with the Pythons did not actually begin or end there, however. Innes, part of the legendary Bonzo Dog (Doo Dah) Band, had performed with that group on the television show *Do Not Adjust Your Set* when Palin, Jones, Idle, and Gilliam were working on that show. Innes was later asked to do some audience warm-ups for the TV series because he was friendly with the group members. Most significant, he acted and wrote songs for *Monty Python and the Holy Grail* and became an important part of the Python stage shows, firmly establishing his Python credentials.

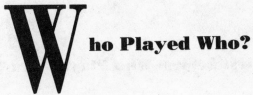

Who Played Who?

Throughout their career, the Pythons have been called upon to portray a dazzling variety of memorable characters ranging from medieval knights to upper-class twits, from legions of Roman soldiers to a gaggle of Gumbys.

So successful have they been that they have often buried themselves within their roles, so that John Cleese virtually *becomes* Attila the Hun and Michael Palin *is* Arthur Putey.

The object of this quiz is to separate the six Pythons from their onscreen characters and determine which of the Pythons (along with Carol Cleveland) played which roles.

Hint: Terry Gilliam seldom appeared on camera early in the TV shows, but his parts increased with each series. Conversely, John Cleese did not appear at all in the fourth series.

The Players:

Graham Chapman
John Cleese
Terry Gilliam

Eric Idle
Terry Jones
Michael Palin
and
Carol Cleveland

The First Series: Who Played Who?

1. Arthur "Two-Sheds" Jackson	17. Mungo the Cook
2. Marriage Guidance Counselor	18. Deidre Putey
3. Ernest Scribbler	19. Superintendent Parrot
4. Mr. Praline	20. Dino Vercotti
5. Marcel Marceau	21. Arthur Name
6. Angus Podgorny	22. Ron Obvious
7. Arthur Frampton	23. Mr. Hilter
8. Sandy Camp	24. Judge
9. Sir George Head, O.B.E.	25. Arthur Lemming of the BDA
10. David Unction	26. Assistant Chief Constable Theresamanbehindyou
11. Ali Bayan	27. Wally Wiggins
12. Professor Tiddles of Leeds University	28. Samuel Brainsample
13. Inspector Harry H. "Snapper" Organs of H Division	29. The Big Cheese
14. Prof. R. J. Canning	30. Professor Gert van der Whoops
15. Mozart	31. Mr. Notlob
16. Harold Larch	32. Arthur Tree (voice)
	33. Mr. Anchovy
	34. Mr. Lambert

The Second Series: Who Played Who?

1. The Bishop
2. Mr. Devious
3. Ken Clean-Air Systems
4. L. F. Dibley
5. Raymond Luxury-Yacht
6. Roy Spim
7. Vanilla Hoare
8. Alexander Yahlt
9. Justice Maltravers
10. Arthur Figgis (village idiot)
11. Arthur Figgis (TV star)
12. Robin Attila the Hun
13. Herbert Mental
14. Man with a Stoat Through His Head
15. Mrs. G. Pinnet
16. Ewan McTeagle
17. BALPA Spokesman
18. Mrs. Nellie Clean-Air Systems
19. Gavin Millarrrrrrrrrr
20. Kevin Pillips-Bong
21. Lady Partridge
22. Dreary Fat Boring Old Git
23. Mrs. Scum
24. Martin Curry
25. Gerry Schlick
26. Sergeant Duckie
27. Cardinal Fang
28. Mrs. April Simnel
29. Shoplifter
30. Superintendent Harry "Snapper" Organs of Q Division
31. Rev. Morrison
32. Kirk Vilb

The Third Series: Who Played Who?

1. Brian Norris
2. Betty Norris
3. Hamrag Yatlerot
4. Anne Elk
5. Henry Wensleydale
6. Philip Jenkinson
7. Arthur Mee
8. Queen Elizabeth
9. Erik Njorl
10. Beulagh Premise
11. Michael Norman Randall
12. Reg Pither
13. Don Roberts
14. Dr. E. Henry Thripshaw
15. Miles Yellowbird
16. George Bernard Shaw
17. The Amazing Mystico
18. Mr. Gulliver
19. Mr. Atkinson
20. Dennis Moore
21. Rev. Ronald Simms, the Dirty Vicar
22. Mr. Akwekwe

13

23. Gumby Brain Specialist
24. Lieutenant Commander Dorothy Lamour
25. Police Constable Pan-Am
26. Mr. Bounder of Adventure
27. McKamikaze Highlander Sapper MacDonald
28. James McNeill Whistler
29. Sir Philip Sidney
30. Mr. Spare-Buttons-Supplied-with-the-Shirt

The Fourth Series: Who Played Who?

1. Chris Quinn
2. Sapper Walters
3. Hamlet
4. Mr. Gabriello
5. Kevin Garibaldi
6. Mr. Neutron
7. Jacques Montgolfier
8. George III
9. Dr. Bruce Genuine
10. Captain Carpenter
11. Mrs. Smoker
12. Mrs. Non-Gorilla
13. Ferdinand von Zeppelin
14. Arab Boy/Channel Changer
15. Supreme Commander of Land, Sea, and Air Forces
16. Percy Shelley
17. Queen Victoria

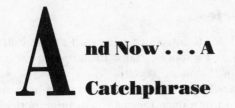

And Now . . . A Catchphrase

The phrase "And now for something completely different" was commonly used by the BBC prior to Python, and when the group itself started using it on the TV shows, it was halfway through the first series before they realized they had somehow appropriated it as their own silly catchphrase.

Apparently devised by John Cleese and Graham Chapman to link sketches, it came to be delivered by John in a variety of situations. He was usually behind a desk, wearing a dinner jacket, and would announce the phrase just prior to the "It's" Man and the opening titles in the second and third series (he was sandwiched between a nude Terry Jones playing the organ and the "It's" Man in series 3 and only said, "And now"). There are those who suspect it is one of John's favorite Python roles because it did not require him to dress up in a peculiar costume or roll around in filth. . . .

Although the phrase is identified with John, Eric Idle and Michael Palin were actually the first ones to deliver it. It came to be identified so strongly with the group that many of the first newspaper articles used the phrase at some point when writing about the group.

And now for—the temptation is hard to resist. Rather—and now, a listing of the ways the phrase is used throughout the TV shows.

First Series

1. Used (by Eric Idle) to introduce a man with three buttocks.
2. Used (by Eric) a few minutes later to introduce the Continental version of that same sketch.
3. Used (by Michael Palin) later in that same show in an unsuccessful attempt to introduce the man with three buttocks.
4. Used by the man in the dinner jacket (in his first appearance), sitting at his desk behind Ada's Snack Bar, to introduce a man with a tape recorder up his nose.
5. Used a few moments later to introduce the office of Sir George Head.
6. Used by two men in dinner jackets at two desks (both played by John) to introduce a man with a tape recorder up his brother's nose.
7. Used by the man in the dinner jacket, sitting at his desk (which is in a chicken coop), to introduce the Visitors Sketch.

Second Series

Unless otherwise noted, used by the man in the dinner jacket to introduce the opening titles; the location of the desk varies.

8. Used by the man in the dinner jacket to introduce the opening titles (for the first time); his desk is in a cage at the zoo.
9. Used at a desk at the base of a cliff, next to wreckage of would-be fliers.
10. Used at a desk on a window washer's platform outside a high-rise window, where a woman is undressing.
11. Used at a desk with propellers that flies into some animation.
12. At the end of "The Buzz Aldrin Show," a group of Gumbys deliver the line and are changed into female Gumbys.
12.½ In show #19, the man in the dinner jacket, at a desk in a blacksmith's shop, explains that he *won't* be saying, "And now for something completely different," because he isn't in that week's show.

16

13. Used at a desk superimposed over stock footage of Huns attacking on horseback.
14. Used by an offscreen announcer (Eric Idle) after several previews of upcoming BBC programs as "And now for something completely different—sport," followed by opening titles.
15. Used by the man in the dinner jacket, who is actually wearing a bikini, after a camera passes by several women in bikinis.
16. Used at the desk at the seashore after Carol Cleveland's clothes have been torn off while running past cacti.
17. The man at the desk becomes stuck, repeating "Completely diff . . . completely diff . . . completely diff . . ."
18. Used at a desk on the coast during the film "The Black Eagle."
18½ *Not* used; the man stands in front of his desk and says he won't be using the phrase as he doesn't think it's fit, since the queen will be tuning in to the show later that evening.

Third Series

Generally used only in shortened form ("And now") following the organ fanfare and prior to the "It's" Man and opening titles; the desk is on a balcony over a village, in a field, or in a boxing ring.
19. The man in the dinner jacket is behind his desk in the middle of a field, being interviewed by reporters; he explains his theories of laughter before saying, "And now . . ."

NOTE: The character and the phrase do not appear at all in the fourth series (nor does John Cleese).

The Dead Parrot War: Mr. Praline vs. The Pet Shop Owner

During the famed battle, Mr. Praline attempts to return a parrot to the shop where he purchased it not half an hour ago. But Praline and the Shopkeeper exchange conflicting viewpoints concerning the condition of the Norwegian Blue.

Listed below are the varying descriptions of the bird. The challenge is to separate Praline's descriptions of the bird from those of the Shopkeeper.

Definitely deceased	Meet its maker
Pining (for the fiords)	Bleeding demised
Kipping (on its back)	Expired
Pushing up the daisies	Ex-parrot
Tired and shagged out	Stunned
Joined the choir invisible	Ceased to be
Rung down the curtain	Is no more
Not pining	Resting
Stiff	Passed on
Bereft of life	Rests in peace

The Upper-Class Twit of the Year Show: The Events

1. Walking a straight line
2. The matchbox jump (over three layers of boxes)
3. Kicking the beggar
4. The Hunt Ball photograph
5. Reversing the sports car into the old woman
6. Waking the neighbor (by slamming the car door)
7. Insulting the waiter
8. Getting under the bar (a wooden bar five feet off the ground)
9. Shooting the rabbit (which is tied to the ground)
10. Taking the bra off the debutante
11. Shooting yourself

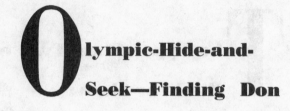 Olympic-Hide-and-Seek—Finding Don Roberts

The second leg of the Olympic final of the Men's Hide-and-Seek is underway, with Francisco Huron of Paraguay seeking Don Roberts of Hinckley in Leicestershire. But, Huron needs your help. Below are the various places where the Paraguayan is looking for Roberts; Huron needs you to match up the locations with the appropriate clues in order to beat the world record time of 11 years, 2 months, 26 days, 9 hours, 3 minutes, and 27.4 seconds.

1. Madagascar	a. Desperately cold
2. Budapest	b. Cold
3. Sardinia	c. Warmer
4. Tagus Valley	d. Correct!
5. Lisbon	

BONUS: Where did Don Roberts find Francisco Huron in the first leg of the competition?

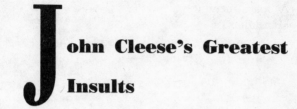

John Cleese's Greatest Insults

Of all the Pythons, John Cleese is perhaps the best at conveying anger, a skill that he later perfected as Basil Fawlty. During Python, however, he was still able to score a number of insults, several of which are listed below. The challenge here, however, is to match the classic Cleese insult with its target.

1. "You bastards! You vicious, heartless bastards!"
2. ". . . You stupid, furry, bucktoothed gits!"
3. "Button your lip, you ratbag!"
4. "You excrement! You lousy hypocritical whining toadies with your lousy color TV sets and your Tony Jacklin golf clubs . . ."
5. ". . . You miserable little man . . . do your worst, you worm!"
6. "You stupid, interfering little rat! Damn your lemon curd tartlet!"
7. "I unclog my nose in your direction . . . I wave my private parts at your aunties, you cheesey-lover second-hand election donkey-bottom biters!"
8. "You stupid, birdbrained, flatheaded . . ."

a. A recruit attacking him with a raspberry
b. The rats living in his (Beethoven's) piano
c. A couple in a restaurant who have been given a dirty fork
d. Brian of Nazareth
e. His wife, Audrey Equator
f. King Arthur and his Knights
g. A board meeting
h. Mr. Pither

pplause

One of the most traditional conventions of most TV variety shows is a cutaway shot of the studio audience applauding, a traditional image that the Pythons decided to include in the *Flying Circus*.

In typical Python fashion, they did not utilize the real studio audience. Instead, they found a stock film clip in the BBC library of an audience applauding. However, this was black-and-white footage of a group of older ladies, the type of which would be found at a women's institute meeting.

Naturally, this bizarre clip was inserted into a number of the TV shows, so that the ladies would apparently be applauding the types of things they would not normally be expected to appreciate.

As wonderfully peculiar as the shot of the older ladies appeared, Michael Palin says that in the earliest days of Python, it was not that far removed from reality. He says that when the group was recording their first TV shows and no one knew what the show was about, the audiences that the BBC assembled for them looked much more like those older ladies in the film than they had ever imagined and weren't always as enthusiastic as they had hoped.

Fortunately, they had the film of the women's institute audience clapping their hands, footage that was used in all four seasons. Below is a list of the things that made them applaud, in order of appearance.

First Series

1. A man with two noses
2. A Scotsman on a horse
3. A man with two noses blowing his elbow
4. The Compere at the seaside, introducing the Restaurant Sketch
5. A Scotsman on a horse riding away with a bridegroom
6. A man with a tape recorder up his nose
7. A Police Fairy Story ("Do you want to come back to my place?")
8. The Knight with the rubber chicken hitting the Doctor (of the Me Doctor Sketch)
9. John the Baptist's impersonation of Graham Hill

Second Series

10. A boxer (Terry Gilliam) knocking out a smartly dressed woman who can't remember her name
11. The same boxer knocking out a nun
12. A policeman who breaks wind in a courtroom
13. The Man with a Stoat Through His Head

Third Series

14. A man who is abused by the Royal Sergeant Major and receives a pie in his face, whitewash, etc.
15. Dennis Moore, realizing that he's stealing from the poor and giving to the rich
16. A Mrs. Nesbitt of York, who spotted a loony in 1.8 seconds
17. An incorrect answer on "Spot the Loony"

Fourth Series

18. The Garibaldi family, contestants on "The Most Awful Family in Britain"

L ook Who's Talking

The talk show (or chat show, for aspiring Anglophiles) was a cherished Python tradition, not least because it provided a convenient format to present characters and parodies. One of the aspects of *Monty Python's Flying Circus* that pleased Graham Chapman the most is that the Pythons were among the first to use the television medium to explore and attack the hand that was feeding it, completely on its own turf, exploiting its own shortcomings.

One of the easiest targets proved to be that venerable TV staple, the talk show. The few Python shows that did not include some sort of talk show usually contained a takeoff on a similar TV institution like the game show, the documentary, or perhaps the sports broadcast.

Listed below are the titles of many of the strangest Python talk shows and the topics of discussion; the object is to match them up. *NOTE:* some of them may apply to more than one show, or vice versa. But, time to stop all this chatting and get to work . . .

"Spectrum" "Party Political Broadcast"
"It's a Tree" "The Money"
"It's" "The Toad Elevating
"World Forum" Moment"
"The Bols Story" "Election Night Special"
"Probe" "Timmy Williams' Coffee
"Thrust" Time"
"Archaeology Today" "Party Hints by Veronica"
"The Great Debate" "Grandstand"
"Farming Club" "The Epilogue"
"How to Do It"
"It's the Arts"
"Face the Press"
"Is There?"
"Blood, Devastation, Death, War, and Horror"

1. Discusses the height of the guests
2. Discusses Arthur J. Smith and Jethro Q. Walrustitty
3. A minister of the Wood party falls through the earth's crust
4. A friend of the star's tries to speak to him about his wife's recent death
5. A monsignor and a humanist grapple over the existence of God.
6. An unusual guest is a piece of laminated plastic.
7. Features one guest who says things in a very roundabout way and other guests who say only parts of words
8. Includes a song about international currency
9. Discusses how to deal with an armed Communist uprising
10. Features anagrams and gardening
11. Examines the unfairness of bullfighting
12. The three guests are all dead.
13. Explores the advantages of voting Norwegian
14. Includes an examination of wifeswapping
15. Discusses another TV channel
16. Features a theory on the brontosaurus
17. Guests are Ringo Starr and Lulu
18. Includes an explanation of pausing and gesturing while speaking
19. Guests are Karl Marx, Che Guevara, Lenin, and Mao Tse-tung

26

20. Looks at the life of Tchaikovsky
21. Explains the way to rid the world of all known diseases
22. The Minister for Home Affairs debates a patch of brown liquid.
23. Features interviews with Arthur "Two-Sheds" Jackson and director Sir Edward Ross
24. Examines what is going on with charts, graphs, etc.
25. Features a man with three buttocks

Going over Like a Sixteen-Ton Weight

Like a lead balloon, it hovers over the heads of the unwary, ready to squash the idiots and twits below. And, like the giant hammer that would come out of nowhere and strike the heads of the unwary, it is like a piece of Terry Gilliam's animation come to life.

Yes, it's the sixteen-ton weight, the giant, cartoony prop the Pythons would use when their patience was at an end and their frustration was at a peak—not unlike the giant foot that would plop down at the end of the opening titles of the TV show. Graham Chapman said the sixteen-ton weight came from their not knowing how to end a revue and hoping for a gigantic boot to come down and smash everything.

Nevertheless, the sixteen-ton weight appeared throughout all but the fourth series of the TV show, and its targets included a variety of persons, listed below.

First Series

1. Mr. Thompson, the recruit attacking the Royal Sergeant Major with a raspberry (the weight is dropped in self-defense)
2. The "Spectrum" host, who is beginning to ramble on
3. Marcel Marceau, who mimes a man being struck about the head by a sixteen-ton weight

Second Series

4. A man who complains about people complaining
5. A vicar performing a wedding in "The Bishop" (the wedding ring is tied to a string, which is tied to the weight)
6. The presenter who has just shown the football match between the Bournemouth Gynecologists and the Watford Long John Silver Impersonators

Third Series

7. A Pantomime Horse, who has it dropped on him by another Pantomime Horse behind a tree
8. Mr. Robinson, after a visit from his neighbors, the Cheap-Laughs
9. Mr. Badger, when he has finished reading the closing credits for one of the shows

Utterly Useless Flying Circus Facts

CLERGYMAN

Rev. Arthur Belling of St. Loony Up the Cream Bun and Jam appears twice in Python—once as he delivers an appeal for sanity in the second series and once as a vicar who disturbs a young couple in the third series. He was played by Graham Chapman in the former sketch and by Michael Palin in the latter.

MRS. SCUM ALSO RISES

Terry Jones played two women named Mrs. Scum—once in the "Spot the Brain Cell" quiz show in the second series and again in the fourth series as a housewife who falls in love with Mr. Neutron.

NO FOOLING

The character called Arthur Figgis appears twice on the Python TV shows. The first time, he presents "It's the Arts" and is played by Graham Chapman; his later appearance is as a village idiot, played by John Cleese.

THE ART OF NAMES

Monty Python's Flying Circus features twenty-six different characters named Arthur; it is by far the name most often used. Runner-up is Ken, used for eighteen different characters.

JUDGMENTS

Judges were portrayed in fourteen different Python sketches (including the presiding general at Sapper Walters's court-martial); of those, Terry Jones was featured as a judge seven times.

Fifty-one different policemen were featured in Python sketches—more than any other occupation; Graham Chapman portrayed a police inspector sixteen of those times.

CLIMB EVERY MOUNTAIN

There were three different mountaineering sketches used in the Python TV series, undoubtedly due in some part to Graham Chapman, who was an experienced mountaineer. One featured a man applying for an expedition with Sir George Head, who sees double; another spotlighted the hairdressers' expedition on Mt. Everest; and the third featured a group attempting to climb the Uxbridge Road.

"IT'S THE ARTS"

The Pythons used "It's the Arts" in two different shows to present different bits. One involved interviews with several show business figures, including Sir Edward Ross; the other featured a look at composer Johann Gambolputty.

AT LAST, THE MARTY FELDMAN SKETCH

The Insurance Sketch at the end of the second series, according to the TV scripts, features characters named Martin and Feldman (several of the Pythons had written for and worked with Marty Feldman prior to Python; Graham Chapman's *Yellowbeard* marked Feldman's last film appearance).

STOP ME IF YOU'VE HEARD THIS ONE

Two separate sketches performed by the Pythons used an identical punch line—the Art Gallery Sketch (from the first TV series) and the Last Supper Sketch (which actually predates Python and was performed with Eric Idle as Michelangelo and John Cleese as the Pope in *Monty Python Live at the Hollywood Bowl*).

They both end with the line "I don't know much about art, but I know what I like."

THE GATHERING STORM

Two Python sketches were subtitled "The Gathering Storm," which is also the title of the first of Winston Churchill's World War II memoirs. One of the Python versions deals with the highwayman Dennis Moore, however, and the other with penguins.

The Ridiculously Trivial Monty Python's Flying Circus Quiz

Section One: Mostly Easy Questions

Monty Python fans are often closer to fanatics. They pride themselves on knowing the most minute details of the sketches and films and delight in repeating favorite lines to the bemusement—and sometimes bewilderment—of friends and family. The various questions in this quiz range from the amazingly easy to the ridiculously difficult.

Of course, it all leads off with the amazingly easy bits. This section is designed to build false confidence in more marginal Python fans and to allow the hard-core fanatics to warm up their Curry's own brains.

Mostly Easy Questions: The First Series

1. How many sheds are owned by Arthur "Two-Sheds" Jackson?
2. Nine out of ten British housewives can't tell the difference between Whizzo butter and what kind of animal?

33

3. Which type of farm animals are under the misapprehension that they're birds?
4. What kind of tableware does the diner complain about that gets the restaurant staff so upset?
5. The Royal Sergeant Major teaches self-defense against assailants armed with what types of weapons?
6. When the suburban couple's cat becomes too complacent, who do they call?
7. An encyclopedia salesman is let into a home by pretending he is a what?
8. Which type of candy in the Whizzo Quality Assortment still has the bones in it?
9. Who turns the population of England into Scotsmen?
10. Which is the worst tennis-playing nation in the world?
11. The newlywed couple is told to ask for dog kennels when they intend to buy what?
12. What type of animal is the Norwegian Blue?
13. Who is the gang that attacks young men and women?
14. The Spanish guitarist and dancer sing about which animal?
15. What has the homicidal barber always wanted to be?
16. Mr. Anchovy, who hopes to become a lion tamer, is actually a member of which profession?
17. Where does Ron Obvious hope to become the first man to jump?
18. Which World War II battle does the Batley Townswomen's Guild choose to reenact?
19. The matchbox jump, kicking the beggar, insulting the waiter, and taking the bra off the debutante are all events in what competition?
20. Who does the doctor find in Mr. Notlob during surgery?
21. The ice-cream seller at intermission is actually trying to sell what sort of bird?

Mostly Easy Questions: The Second Series

1. Who are the two gangster brothers whose tactics include nailing their victims' heads to the floor?
2. National Defense receives more government funding than which British ministry?
3. What are the three chief weapons of the Spanish Inquisition?

4. The strange feeling we sometimes get that we've lived through something before is called what?
5. The architect who mainly designs slaughterhouses is more interested in joining which organization?
6. What is the name of the game show that features a nude man playing the organ and a Stop the Film segment?
7. Who is the boxer who has his head sawed off to wake him up and fights schoolgirl Petula Wilcox?
8. Which film of L. F. Dibley's was called similar to Stanley Kubrick's identically titled movie?
9. How is Raymond Luxury-Yacht pronounced?
10. To which political party does Jethro Q. Walrustitty belong?
11. "A Tale of Two Cities," adapted by Joey Boy, is presented for what type of animal?
12. An animated table of food is attacked by what dinner roll?
13. Mrs. Scum wins a blow on the head on a TV quiz show with the answer "Reginald Maudling." What question was she answering?
14. Which profession is Colin "Chopper" Mozart (the son of the composer) in?
15. Who is Mrs. Dreary Fat Boring Old Git married to?
16. What are most of the people in the philosophy department of the University of Woolamaloo named?
17. Where is the exploding penguin located?
18. Because there are no lions in the Antarctic, the title of "Scott of the Antarctic" is changed to what?
19. Mr. Praline, who tries to buy a license for his fish, has given all his pets the same name. What is it?
20. Which corporation is headed by Arthur Crackpot?
21. Who are the four figures that answer questions about English football on "World Forum?"
22. What food do Vikings sing about?
23. What do the five sailors in the lifeboat decide to eat?

Mostly Easy Questions: The Third Series

1. "Njorl's Saga," which later takes place in Malden, is originally set in what country?
2. Who is the French writer and philosopher visited by Mrs. Premise and Mrs. Conclusion?

3. Which Russian classical composer is featured on "Farming Club"?
4. Who tries to establish a link between the inhabitants of Hounslow and Surbiton?
5. The room for abuse is next door to which other room?
6. What pantomime animal is featured as a secret agent battling his Soviet counterpart?
7. Contestants in swimsuits and evening dresses must summarize which writer?
8. Teams of international hairdressers, French chiropodists, and the Glasgow Orpheus Male Voice Choir try to climb what mountain?
9. Who is the complaining man that visits the travel agent (and can't say the letter *C*)?
10. Which prehistoric animal does Anne Elk have a theory about?
11. What does a door-to-door documentary presenter feature in the program he does in a living room?
12. Who is the fictional World War I pilot, with a sidekick named Algy, who dictates a letter?
13. How many different cheeses does Ye Olde Cheese Emporium have?
14. What happens to the piano player in "Sam Peckinpah's 'Salad Days'?"
15. Who is on a cycling tour of North Cornwall and ends up in Moscow?
16. Who is the cyclist's companion, who is transformed into Clodagh Rogers, Trotsky, Eartha Kitt, and Edward Heath?
17. Which Olympic event took 11 years, 2 months, 26 days, 9 hours, 3 minutes, and 27.4 seconds to complete?
18. Who is the conjurer, assisted by Janet, who can put up an entire block of flats by hypnosis?
19. What kind of books and magazines does the Tudor Job Agency actually deal in?
20. What new disease is discovered by Dr. E. Henry Thripshaw?
21. Who is the highwayman that robs the nobility of their lupins?
22. What is the name of the highwayman's horse?
23. Which phrase inspired a series based on the wild and lawless days of the post-Impressionists?
24. What substance does the donor wish to give instead of blood?

Mostly Easy Questions: The Fourth Series

1. Who made the first ascent in a hot air balloon?
2. What type of pet does Chris Quinn return to the department store?
3. Who is it that the department store keeps paging and Chris Quinn is often mistaken for?
4. Which sporting event involves the casts of "The Sound of Music," "Oklahoma," and "Ben-Hur"?
5. Who wrote "Anything Goes"?
6. What does Hamlet tell his psychiatrist he really wants to be?
7. Mr. Gabriello, the boxing manager, keeps what in a bag after the champ's match?
8. Who is the retired CIA agent that breeds rabbits in the Yukon?
9. What contest does the Garibaldi family compete in?

The Complete and Utter History of the Opening Titles

The animated titles that begin the TV shows were one of the few concessions the group made to conventionality—even though they soon began using them in as unconventional a manner as possible.

Nearly all the shows used opening titles animated by Terry Gilliam, although they were seldom run at the opening of the shows. As might be expected of the Pythons, they eventually began appearing in the middle of the shows and even at the end of shows, and some shows did not use the opening titles at all. One show featured the titles at the beginning of a show, immediately followed by the closing credits: anything to thumb their collective noses at conventionality.

For hard-core Python fans, the titles serve another purpose—when the shows feature the opening animation, they are a rather accurate indication of the season that particular show was taped.

All thirteen shows in the first series feature Michael Palin as the "It's" Man, saying, "It's," just before the titles roll. Most of

38

the shows in the second series use John Cleese, wearing a dinner jacket and sitting behind a desk, saying, "And now for something completely different," followed by Michael Palin's "It's" and the animated titles. The third series titles usually begin with a nude Terry Jones playing an organ fanfare, followed by Cleese's "And now for something completely different" and Palin's "It's." The fourth series shows were simply called *Monty Python,* with the *Flying Circus* half apparently going the way of John Cleese (who left the show at the end of the third season).

Terry Gilliam's opening animation changed along the way as well. Although all the normal openings and closings featured John Philip Sousa's "Liberty Bell," Gilliam created new titles for the third series and then another new sequence for the final season.

The titles were played fairly straight in the first series, with all shows involving the "It's" Man prior to the animation.

By the second series, the group began loosening up a bit more; in the middle of that series, in the show that begins with "It's a Living," there is no "It's" Man or "And now for something completely different." Instead, the animated titles begin in the dark, and a light switch is thrown on in the middle of them.

For the final show of the second season, Terry devised an entirely new set of animated titles. Since the theme of the evening was that the queen was going to be tuning in sometime during the show, the Pythons announce they will be carrying on "completely as normal." Naturally, the titles that follow are all very regal and are accompanied by "God Save the Queen."

A completely new set of titles was devised for the third series, although they were not used at all in "Cycling Tour," the Palin/Jones half-hour sequence.

The fourth series also featured a completely new animated opening, although the opening titles were not used at all in the first show, "The Golden Age of Ballooning." The other shows generally used the beginning sequence with no introduction, although the third show of that series did feature a nude Terry Jones at the organ and the "It's" Man prior to the titles.

Tips for Self-defense

In one of the most important early Python sketches, John Cleese instructs a group of raw recruits in self-defense. As a public service, the various types of fresh fruit used as weapons are listed below, along with the proper type of defense to be used against them.

Match the various weapons with the method of defense to be used against them and, for extra credit, identify which one was not demonstrated in the sketch. Those being attacked by a homicidal maniac with a bunch of loganberries or a pointed stick are on their own.

1. Bananas	a. Release the tiger
2. Peach	b. Shoot the assailant and eat the fruit
3. Raspberry	c. Drop a sixteen-ton weight
4. Bunch of raspberries	d. Release the crocodile

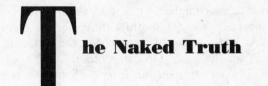

The Naked Truth

None of the Pythons have had any qualms about taking off their clothes when duty calls (or even when it doesn't) for films, TV, or print.

Of course, the all-time Python leader here is Terry Jones, who, sitting at an organ prior to the titles in the third series, wore a fright wig, a frightening grin, and little else. Michael Palin has said that Terry had no compunction about taking his clothes off anywhere, from TV studios to lovely, picturesque little villages (Terry also appeared nude in *Life of Brian*, covered only by a long flowing gray wig, as Simon the Holy Man).

Actually, the first nude organist—used in the second series for "Blackmail"—was played by Terry Gilliam, who also wore a very small loincloth and plenty of mud playing a blood-and-thunder prophet in *Life of Brian*.

It was in *Brian* that the most graphic Python nudity took place. It was full frontal nudity for Graham Chapman when, the morning after an evening with Judith, he threw open his window and a huge crowd was inadvertently exposed to his assets. Although Graham wasn't eager to do the scene, he had resigned himself to it, even though some of the crowd members were taken aback.

Many of the hundreds of extras assembled in the courtyard were Muslim, and it is forbidden for Muslim women to see such male nudity. Apparently, many of the extras hadn't been adequately briefed on what to expect.

Therefore, when a completely naked Graham threw open the windows to the courtyard for the first time, he was greeted by scattered shrieks and screams of terror. "Not the sort of reaction that does much for the ego," Graham noted.

Michael Palin once stripped for Terry Gilliam. No, it's not a tabloid headline, but when Michael was starring in *Jabberwocky,* one scene had him standing in a line outside a castle and removing his clothes to get in (which doesn't work).

It was in non-Python films that John Cleese took off his clothes (in addition to his *Meaning of Life* role as the teacher who delivers the sex lecture). Most Cleese fans are probably familiar with the hilarious strip John does in *A Fish Called Wanda,* when he is preparing to bed Jamie Lee Curtis and is surprised by an upper-middle-class family. What many people don't know is that it was Jamie who was supposed to do that scene, until she pointed out to John that it would be much funnier if he was the one caught naked. John agreed immediately and rewrote the scene.

John also appeared nude in a short film he did with then-wife Connie Booth just prior to working on *Fawlty Towers* with her. In fact, both of them appeared nude throughout nearly all of 1974's *Romance with a Double Bass.*

Eric Idle appeared nude in "The Vatican Sex Manual" for his *Rutland Dirty Weekend Book,* demonstrating, with a similarly unclad lady, the sexual positions approved by the Vatican; an excerpt from this was also published in *Playboy.*

During *Monty Python Live at the Hollywood Bowl,* Chapman, Cleese, Gilliam, and Jones appeared in period costumes with long aprons down the front to sing "Sit on My Face." When they turned to walk offstage, however, their underwear had been removed, and the four of them mooned the audience.

Finally, when Pythonmania started in the United States in the mid-1970s, photographer Richard Avedon was scheduled to photograph the group (although John Cleese "wasn't available"). The remaining five joked that Avedon would want to shoot them in the nude—which he did (the photo was later reprinted in the *Life of Brian* book). They managed to cover their naughty bits, although an enthusiastic Terry Jones managed to pose upside down . . .

All of which would go to show, it seems, that Monty Python has nothing to hide . . .

Titles and Topics: The Python Documentary Quiz

*M*onty Python's Flying Circus includes a number of wonderful documentaries and educational programs throughout the forty-five shows, segments that inform as well as entertain.

They deal with a variety of subjects, ranging from crime to life-and-death struggles of wildlife to the sexual perversions of mollusks. Some of them never get made, such as the one dealing with the homeless living in the street (the camera crew is chased off and told to do a program on the drug problem on Walton Street). There are other times in which two documentaries are occurring simultaneously, so the presenter of the profile of Sir Walter Scott must battle with the announcer of the forestry program for control of one microphone.

The completed documentaries are listed below in order of their appearance on the TV shows; the object of the documentary quiz is to match the name of the program with the subject matter dealt with (*NOTE:* "It's the Arts" has contained both talk-show segments and documentary profiles—this quiz involves the documentary material only).

Titles

1. "The World Around Us"
2. "It's the Arts"
3. "The World of History"
4. "Probe Around"
5. "Ethel the Frog"
6. "It's the Mind"
7. "The Wonderful Timmy Williams"
8. "Tomorrow's World"
9. "Fish Club"
10. "Whicker's World"
11. "Mr. and Mrs. Brian Norris's Ford Popular"
12. "War Against Pornography"
13. "Storage Jars"
14. "Frontiers of Medicine," Part Two—The Gathering Storm
15. "University of the Air"
16. "Nationwide"

Topics

a. Animal communication and the anatomy of ants
b. Bolivian storage jars
c. Crime and the use of magic by the police force
d. The violence of the British gangland and the Piranha brothers
e. A theory that the penguin is more intelligent than humans
f. A super prize-winning documentary on the beloved TV star
g. An island inhabited by former international interviewers
h. The Mouse Problem—what makes a man want to be a mouse
i. An anthropological journey between Hounslow and Surbiton
j. How to feed a goldfish
k. The Black Death and social legislation in the 18th century
l. A newsreel of Mrs. Britain tilting at the permissive society
m. Political groupies
n. The theory that sitting down regularly in a comfortable chair can rest your legs
o. A profile of the greatest name in German baroque music
p. The phenomenon of deja vu

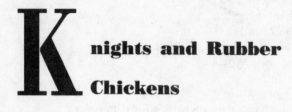Knights and Rubber Chickens

The Pythons used a number of characters and devices, including the Colonel, the Viking, and the women's institute applause, to link sketches that would otherwise have absolutely nothing in common.

Certainly one of the most peculiar linking characters was the Knight. Long before *Holy Grail,* the Knight would generally walk into a sketch, hit a character over the head with a rubber chicken, then turn and walk off.

Laurence Olivier probably would have refused the part, but not Terry Gilliam. The director-to-be was wrapped up in his animation at the time, but he had very little to do the days the shows were taped. Since he would get bored just sitting around—and also because he felt rather inadequate performing with the other five—Terry would look for smaller, silly bits to do. And one of those was the Knight. Gilliam claimed the part as his own, since none of the others were exactly clamoring to be closed up in the armor, and thus had his first recurring bit onscreen in the TV shows.

As the series progressed, however, Terry became less and less reluctant to attempt more ambitious roles, and after the end of the first series, the Knight virtually became a thing of the past.

The Knight's Targets

(All in series 1 unless otherwise noted)

1. Hits Arthur Putey over the head with his rubber chicken at the end of the Marriage Guidance Counselor Sketch
2. Hits Mr. Bartlett (the attorney) over the head at the end of the courtroom scene, just after Bartlett has finished singing, "If I were not before the bar, something else I'd like to be . . ."
3. The man from the Dirty Fork Sketch borrows the chicken and hits the compere at the seaside
4. An early version of Mr. Gumby (played by John Cleese) during a Vox Pops on customs regulations—he covers his head, and the Knight hits him in the stomach
5. The interviewer who has just been talking about camel spotting
6. A police inspector warning viewers about blancmanges (actually, the camera cuts away just before the Knight strikes him)
7. No one—just after the hunting film, the Knight, standing by expectantly, is told that he isn't needed that week
8. A doctor, just following the Me Doctor Sketch
9. A red-coated compere at the seaside is struck by Mr. Robinson, who then hands the chicken to the Knight as he walks off to begin the Cheap-Laughs Sketch. This show in the third series is the Knight's only appearance after the first series ends.

Nobody Expects the Spanish Inquisition Quiz

In the early years of the 1970s, to combat the rising tide of religious unorthodoxy, the BBC gave Monty Python of London leave to move without let or hindrance throughout the land, in a reign of violence, terror, and torture that makes a smashing TV series. This resulted in the Spanish Inquisition Sketch . . .

Actually, the skit came about during a Michael Palin/Terry Jones writing session. Michael recalls having written the line "I didn't expect a kind of Spanish Inquisition," so naturally they realized that the Spanish Inquisition obviously had to enter the scene at that point. The diabolical Spaniards then appeared at several crucial points during the show, becoming a fan favorite.

1. Who expects the Spanish Inquisition?
2. What are the four—no, five—chief weapons of the Spanish Inquisition?
3. What are the three methods of torture used on their victims?
4. How is Lady Mountback tortured?
5. How is the Old Lady tortured?
6. What are the three—no, four—types of heresy that the Old Lady is charged with?
7. Who are the two assistants of Cardinal Ximinez?

48

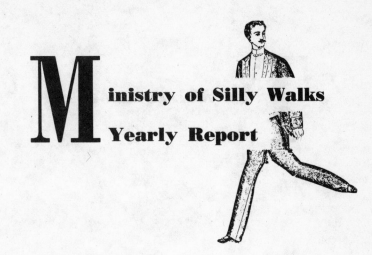

Ministry of Silly Walks
Yearly Report

Annual budget: 348,000,000 pounds sterling (less than national defense, social security, health, housing, and education)

Ongoing research: the Anglo-French Silly Walk *(La Marche Futile)*

Confirmed intelligence reports: Japanese have a man who can bend his leg back over his head and back again with every single step

Rejected grant requests: Mr. Arthur Putey; right leg isn't silly at all, and left leg does a forward aerial half turn every alternate step

Ministry's preferred Silly Walk: little jumps, then three long paces without moving the top of body

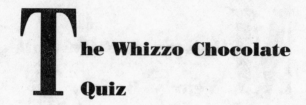

The Whizzo Chocolate Quiz

The Whizzo Quality Assortment contains some of the more unconventional types of confectionery, which came to the attention of Inspector Praline and Superintendent Parrot of the hygiene squad. Listed below are several types of chocolates contained in the assortment, along with a few that Praline thought it should contain. The object of this quiz is to list the sweets used in the Whizzo Quality Assortment—and remember, Whizzo uses no artificial preservatives or additives of any kind!

Cherry Fondue	Lime Cream
Praline	Anthrax Ripple
Spring Surprise	Cockroach Cluster
Almond Whirl	Ram's Bladder Cup
Crunchy Frog	

Monty Python and the Holy Grail Quiz

1. In what language are the subtitles of the opening credits?
2. Who plays Patsy and first bangs the coconuts together?
3. Which type of swallow is large enough to carry a coconut? Why is it unlikely?
4. How much does Eric Idle charge to load a dead body onto his cart?
5. Who disarms the Black Knight?
6. Why do witches burn?
7. Who was the first knight to join King Arthur?
8. What is the first item the French taunters fire in their catapult?
9. How does Sir Robin escape from the Three-Headed Knight?
10. Which castle has a Grail-shaped beacon?
11. What word frightens the Knights Who Say "Ni"?
12. What do the Knights Who Say "Ni" want King Arthur to get for them?
13. Who sends King Arthur and his Knights to the Cave of Caerbannog? Who soils his armor once they get there?
14. How does Sir Gawain die?
15. The old man from scene 24 is also the guardian of what?

Stop It, Stop It, Too Silly . . .

The Colonel is one of the best-loved characters in Python and was one of Graham Chapman's very favorite roles as well. He enjoyed the sense of liberation and power that the part allowed him; he was capable of walking into virtually any ongoing scene to change or stop it entirely, giving orders to the actors and crew in the process. He loved to use the authority to make fun of the real-life colonels as well, and those who try to dominate others.

Although the Colonel figure occasionally acted in regular sketches (such as Joke Warfare, where he first appeared), he was at his most effective walking into sketches (often when the group couldn't think of a punch line) and acting as a link—Graham called playing the Colonel "very liberating."

The role was also one of the few authority figures not played by John Cleese, who was considered within the group to be the logical choice to represent respectable (if slightly twisted) society roles, due to his size and appearance. The few remaining authority figures, usually those more exaggerated (such as the Colonel and Irving C. Saltzberg) tended to go to Graham.

The Colonel appeared in the first series to interrupt the action, but by the second series the group was finding other ways to cut off sketches and start others—so, rather than overuse the Colonel, he appeared very seldom after that. Nevertheless, the Colonel's interruptions in the first series freed the Pythons from the typical conventions of sketch comedy and allowed them to expand from there.

It is significant that as well remembered as the Colonel's appearances on *Monty Python's Flying Circus* are, he only interrupted sketches on *two* shows, although he appeared in full-length sketches on a few other shows as well.

First Series

"Whither Canada?"—The Colonel first appears in the Joke Warfare Sketch, in a fairly straightforward bit in which he describes efforts to produce a German version of the Killer Joke. No interrupting here.

"Owl Stretching Time"—Here, as a caption appears reading "It's a man's life in the Cardiff Rooms, Libya" a singer (Eric Idle) is the target of a protest by the Colonel, who points out that it is too similar to the army's slogan "It's a dog's life . . . a *man's* life in the modern army." He then orders the director to cut away from him.

Shortly after that, the Colonel objects to the caption "It's a man's life taking your clothes off in public," claiming it infringes on the army's copyrighted "It's a pig's life . . . *man's* life in the modern army."

In a later film segment, he interrupts a rustic monologue by John Cleese that begins with "It's a man's life in England's Mountain Green" and chastises the film crew for not doing anything about teeth.

Following a dental sketch that ends with "It's a man's life in the British Dental Association," the Colonel orders the show to stop, which it does.

"Full Frontal Nudity"—This show kicks off with the Army Protection Racket Sketch, in which the Vercotti brothers try to intimidate the Colonel into buying "protection" for his army. He stops the sketch because it's badly written and because he hasn't had a funny line. He orders the director to zoom in on him and he then orders him to cut to a cartoon.

Shortly after the Buying a Bed Sketch, the Colonel warns that the last sketches were getting too silly and notes that "no one likes a good laugh more than I do." Then, he orders up a "good, clean, healthy outdoor sketch," and the director cuts to the Hermits Sketch.

After a few minutes of that, the Colonel then walks onto the hillside. He tells the entire film crew that the sketch is too silly and makes them leave.

When the Dead Parrot Sketch ends and Mr. Praline complains that it's getting too silly, the Colonel walks onto the set next to him and agrees, then orders the director to get on with it.

And as the Hell's Grannies Sketch begins discussing gangs of Keep Left signs, the Colonel walks on. He complains that it's gotten too silly; he also points out that the signs are badly made and the vicar's hair is too long.

Fourth Series

"Anything Goes/The Light Entertainment War"—the Colonel does not appear again until the fourth series. By this time, he has apparently been promoted to General, but it's obviously the same character. He doesn't interrupt any sketches but appears throughout the Trivializing the War scene; he is quite concerned that the enemy is doing very silly things, like dropping cabbages instead of bombs.

Film

Meaning of Life—the Colonel makes his final appearance (wearing combat fatigues) here, immediately following a military scene. He provides a link to the next one as he is struck down while explaining the vital need for the military.

Look Who's Talking

or

The Pythons Say the

Darndest Things Quiz

Python fans can often be recognized by other, normal persons by their propensity for, among other things, interjecting peculiar Python non sequiturs into polite conversation. Still, not all fans can match the lines with the correct characters. Someone who interjects, "If we took the bones out, it wouldn't be crunchy!" into a discussion of medieval agrarian techniques might attract his or her share of attention, but would he or she be able to inform his or her peers that the line was originally spoken by Mr. Milton of Whizzo Chocolate Company?

With that in mind, the quiz below is intended to test your knowledge of the characters created for *Monty Python's Flying Circus*. Match the lines with the characters who said them, and remember, a nod's as good as a wink to a blind bat . . .

The First Series: Lines

1. "I got three cheeks."
2. "Well, everything breaks, don't it, Colonel?"

3. "I should probably have said at the outset that I'm noted for having something of a sense of humor."
4. "Cut, cut, cut, blood, spurt, artery, murder, Hitchcock . . ."
5. "None of this 'pussycat' nonsense?"
6. "Once you've seen one yeti, you've seen them all."
7. "Good evening, Brian."
8. "I'm afraid I must not ask anyone to leave the room."
9. "Curses! I thought I was safe, disguised as Attila the Hun."
10. "Even now, you yourself, you do hardly notice me . . ."
11. ". . . I don't want you to think of the Wood party as a load of old men that like hanging around on ropes."
12. "We are proud to be bringing you one of the evergreen bucket kickers."
13. ". . . Any recurrence of this sloppy, long-haired civilian plagiarism will be dealt with most severely."
14. "The object of this expedition is to see if we can find any traces of last year's expedition."
15. "I'm the special. Try me with some rice."
16. "The plumage don't enter into it."
17. "Sandwiches? Blimey, whatever did I give the wife?"
18. "Funny, isn't it, how naughty dentists always make that one fatal mistake?"
19. "You can tame them after dark, when they're less stroppy."
20. "I want you to think of me as an old queen. *Friend!*"
21. "After five years, they give me a brush."
22. "If there's one thing I can't stand, it's a yes-man!"
23. "Hands off, you filthy bally froggie!"

Ken Biggles	The Barber
Arthur Putey	Jimmy Buzzard
The Colonel	Ken Shabby
Irving C. Saltzberg	Hopkins
Brian Equator	Sir Edward Ross
Mr. Anchovy	Arthur Lemming
Mr. Thomas Walters	Luigi Vercotti
Alexander the Great	Sir George Head
Rt. Hon. Lambert Warbeck	David Unction
Arthur Framptom	Inspector Tiger
Mozart	Mr. Bimmler
Camel Spotter	Mr. Milton
Mr. Praline	Police Constable Henry Thatcher

The Second Series: Lines

1. "The great thing about Ken is that he's almost totally stupid."
2. ". . . Just because he had bloody Grace Kelly, he made three million pounds more than I did."
3. "I noticed a slight look of anxiety cross your face for a moment . . ."
4. "Sea, sand, and sunshine make Paignton the Queen of the English Riviera."
5. "Of course not. It just fell off the wall."
6. "Hello, Sailors!"
7. "Arms out, fingers together, knees bent, now, head well forward. Now, flap your arms!"
8. ". . . You are badly in need of an expensive course of psychiatric treatment."
9. "I hadn't correctly divined your attitude towards your tenants."
10. "Chuff, chuff, chuff, whoooooch, whoooooch!"
11. "Peace? I like a peace. Know what I mean?"
12. "The point is frozen, the beast is late out of Paddington."
13. "I am very proud to be in charge of the first religion with free gifts."
14. "Wonderful to see you, super, super, super . . ."
15. "Give me my nose back!"
16. "I wouldn't kill an animal I didn't like."
17. "But I've never acted out of a trench."
18. "He is an halibut."
19. "Two, er, three to the Old Bailey, please."
20. "Lend us a quid till the end of the week."
21. "I don't think there's a punch line scheduled, is there?"
22. "I want you kids to get a-head."
23. "A really blithering idiot can make anything up to ten thousand pounds a year."
24. "Australia, Australia, Australia, Australia, we love you."
25. "The workers' control of the means of production?"
26. "You have beautiful thighs."
27. "I gave it gladly. I . . . I sang as they sawed it off."
28. ". . . ood . . . ing."
29. "One on't cross beams gone owt askew on treddle."
30. "Ugh! With a gammy leg?"

Attila the Hun	Ewan McTeagle
Mr. Herbert Mental	BBC Man
Raymond Luxury-Yacht	Kirk Vilb
Vanilla Hoare	Hungarian
Archbishop Nudge	Hank Spim
Eric Praline	Mr. Devious
The Milkman	The Butler
Cardinal Ximinez	Bruces
Gavin Millarrrrrrrrr	Karl Marx
Arthur Crackpot	Timmy Williams
Mr. Engelbert	Mr. Anemone
Humperdinck	Reg
Minister of Silly Walks	Neville Shunt
M. Brando	Padre
Thompson	A Sniveling Little Rat-
Chris Conger	Faced Git
Mr. Ohn Ith	Mr. Wiggin (of Ironside &
L. F. Dibley	Malone)
Air Chief Marshall Sir Vincent "Kill the Japs" Forster	

The Third Series: Lines

1. "That's still not grounds for calling me señor, or Don Beegles for that matter."
2. "Well, I feel that they have missed the whole point of my disease."
3. "We've also developed a tomato which can eject itself when an accident is imminent."
4. "I'm sorry, I can't say the letter *B*."
5. "Oh, what is my theory?"
6. "Your Majesty is like a dose of clap."
7. "I'd like to get my fingers around those knockers."
8. "To have murdered so many people in such a short space of time is really awful, and I really am very, very, very sorry that I did it."
9. "We established base salon here, and climbed quite steadily up to Mario's here."
10. "Well, things is pretty bad there at the moment, but there does seem some hope of a constitutional settlement."
11. "So! Phirip's garreons ale hele."
12. "I've just spent four hours burying the cat."

13. "'Toledo Tit Parade'? What sort of play's that?"
14. "I'm afraid we're fresh out of Red Leicester, Sir."
15. "No, no, I am not the brain specialist."
16. "Well, this is a completely uncharted lake, with like hitherto unclassified marine life, man . . ."
17. "No, dear, this is the dream, you're still in the cell."
18. "Your life or your lupins, My Lord."
19. "Now, you were saying, I'm very, very, very, very, very, very, very, very, very, very, very rich."
20. "I'm charging you two under Section 21 of the Strange Sketch Act."
21. "May I recommend the alligator purees?"
22. "It's funny, isn't it? How your best friend can just blow up like that?"
23. "7:30, fed cat. 8:00, breakfast. 8:30, yes (successfully)."
24. "Taht si crreoct."
25. "Would you like drinkee? Or game bingo?"
26. "They are as strong, solid, and as safe as any other building material in this country . . . provided, of course, people *believe* in them."
27. "You're sure I won't be disturbing you?"
28. "These IQ tests were thought to contain an unfair cultural bias against the penguin."

Dr. Lewis Hoad	Mr. Badger
Oscar Wilde	Anne Elk
The Dirty Vicar	Henry Wensleydale
Jeremy Toogood	Bert Tagg
Dennis Moore	Beulagh Premise
Rev. Arthur Belling	Queen Erizabeth
Francisco Huron	Mrs. Shazam
Clement Onan	Akwekwe
Mr. Atkinson	Hamrag Yatlerot
Inspector Gaskell/Sir Philip Sidney	Merchant Banker
	Richard Baker
Inspector Flying Fox of the Yard	Eamonn
	Mr. McGough
Colonel Sir John "Teasy-Weasy" Butler	Mrs. Pither
	Brian Norris
Mr. Gulliver	Gumby Brain Specialist
Biggles	Michael Norman Randall
Sir Jane Russell	Mr. Smoke-Too-Much

The Fourth Series: Lines

1. "The way he kept on fighting after his head came off!"
2. "Mrs. S, I can eat enormous quantities of ice cream without being sick."
3. "When you're king of France, you've got better things to do than go around all day remembering your bloody number!"
4. "What I want to know, Mrs. Elizabeth III, is why they give us crap like that, when there's bits of the Leicester bypass what have never been shown."
5. "Then there's Stanley . . . he's our eldest . . . he's a biochemist in Sutton. He's married to Shirley . . ."
6. "Late in life's pageant it may be . . . but you have made the roses bloom anew for me . . ."
7. "You said you'd clean the tiger out, but do you? No. I suppose you've lost interest in it now."
8. "I am so excited, I could hardly wash."
9. "Bally Jerry pranged his kite right in the how's your father."
10. "I've run out of beans!"
11. "Why does anyone want to be a private dick? Fame, money, glamor, excitement, sex!"
12. "*Antelope*—tinny sort of word . . ."
13. "Oh, dear, I'm not supposed to go mad until 1800!"
14. "Of course I'm not calling it after Bismarck!"
15. "My name is Ozymandias, King of Ants."

Kevin Garibaldi	Hamlet
Ferdinand von Zeppelin	Percy Shelley
Jacques Montgolfier	Mr. Neutron
Chris Quinn's mother	George III
Mrs. Mock Tudor	Squadron Leader
Mrs. Scum	Mansfield
Mrs. Entrail	Louis XIV
Mr. Gabriello	

Blowing up Real Good

The Pythons were somewhat slow to discover the joys of explosions, but once they began blowing things up, they couldn't be stopped. Not content with bits of gunfire and stock footage of explosions, they soon took the same relish in explosions that they enjoyed when dropping sixteen-ton weights on people and objects.

Listed below, in order of appearance, are the items blown up in the course of *Monty Python's Flying Circus*.

First Series

1. A bus driving through an army battle (in "The Dull Life of a City Stockbroker")
2. The "It's" Man (who blows up in the woods after being handed a bomb)
3. An intermission sign

Second Series

1. An elk in a forest
2. An owl in the same forest
3. A lamb in the same forest
4. A cat on a garden wall
5. A rabbit in the forest
6. Unseen objects near a zoo
7. A model of a block of flats
8. Rev. Grundy and his pulpit (in "The Bishop")
9. Rev. Neuk as he performs a baptism
10. The country house in the Accidents Sketch
11. A bank (blown up by outlaw sheep)
12. Fish (blown up with dynamite thrown by Hank and Roy Spim)
13. A penguin on the telly
14. A Webb's Wonder lettuce (from "Le Fromage Grand")
15. Numerous persons during "How Not to Be Seen"
16. Terry Jones, hiding inside a filing cabinet
17. Ground bombed by an animated plane, which results in flowers (leading into "Flower Arrangement")
18. A Madonna balloon carrying a bomb
19. An entire orchestra performing the exploding version of "The Blue Danube"

Third Series

1. The third series animated titles all feature an explosion
2. Mrs. Nigger-Baiter
3. Numerous items explode in the stock footage before "Blood, Devastation, Death, War, and Horror"
4. Mortar bombs fighting the war against pornography
5. An East Scottish Airways plane does *not* explode, although there is a bomb planted in it
6. St. Loony Up the Cream Bun and Jam Church (the sound of an explosion only)
7. An animated head
8. The animated Charwoman

Fourth Series

1. German bombing raid (stock film) during the Banter Sketch
2. Footage of explosions and soldiers in drag during "The Light Entertainment War"
3. A computer (blown up by a nurse)
4. A moor explodes at the end of a show (and Michael Palin walks from the rubble)
5. Cairo, Bangkok, Cape Town, Buenos Aires, Harrow, Hammersmith, Stepney, Wandsworth, and Enfield (in the search for Mr. Neutron)
6. Teddy Salad and two other agents, the Supreme Commander, the Gobi Desert GPO dedication ceremony, and the entire world (in the battle against Mr. Neutron)
7. An animated opera singer, after being shot by a cannon in slow motion

Film

1. The killer rabbit, blown up by the Holy Hand Grenade of Antioch
2. Cliffs, rocks, etc., blown up by Tim the Enchanter

T he Restaurant Sketches Quiz

1. The Jungle Restaurant
2. La Gondola Restaurant
3. Grillomat Snack Bar
4. Eskimo Restaurant
5. Three-Star Restaurant
6. Vegetarian Restaurant
7. The Dungeon Restaurant

a. Customer gets a dirty fork
b. All the spicy pleasures of the Mediterranean
c. The Italian chef can't interest customers in anything but fish
d. The hors d'oeuvres is "Blackmail" and the main course is prawn salad
e. Features chicken a la reine, scampi desiree, and alligator purees
f. Specializes in philosophical conversations
g. The vicar's been sitting for two weeks and nobody's touched him

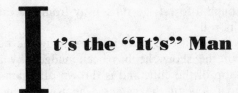

It's the "It's" Man

One of the favorite recurring characters in Python is also one of the first. The so-called "It's" Man seldom gets to say more than that, but he does introduce the opening titles to nearly every TV show in a variety of memorable situations.

As Michael Palin—who played the character in torn, ragged clothing—explains, the "It's" Man was intended to be a one-time smooth TV presenter who had fallen on hard times. Palin always felt that the character had once been allowed to do long, elaborate program announcements but now was allowed to deliver only a one- or two-word introduction.

At any rate, as the shows progressed, the "It's" Man actually had less and less to do on *Monty Python's Flying Circus*. His elaborate sequences prior to the opening titles in the first series eventually gave way to brief close-up insert shots of him saying, "It's," although he did have a few moments to shine. Listed below are all the significant appearances of the character, listed by series.

First Series

Crawling onto a beach; at the end of the show, he is prodded by a stick and crawls back into the water

Running across sand dunes toward the camera as the slamming sound of metal doors is heard

Running through a forest; he runs away from the camera as the closing credits roll

Being thrown from a cliff and crawling along the beach below; at the end of the show, he has been nudged by a stick, has reached the top of the cliff, and is thrown off again

Rowing a boat toward the camera; he rows away during the credits

Running to answer a ringing telephone on a tree stump; at the end of the show, he is on the phone with Irving C. Saltzberg

Racing down a hill and forgetting to say his line/word

Sitting in a lounge chair, sipping wine, and being handed a bomb; at the end of the show, he runs off with the bomb (which explodes off camera)

Running through the woods, followed by explosions; as the closing credits roll, he runs back into the woods and is blown up

Hanging on a meat hook among pig carcasses; he is carried away to the slaughterhouse at the end of the show

Running across the street through heavy traffic; he runs back across during the closing credits

Running through a forest and bouncing off trees like a pinball; he runs back at the end

Being carried in a coffin by four undertakers; he runs from them as the closing credits roll

Second Series

During the second series, the "It's" Man appearances were all before the opening titles and featured just a close-up of him saying his line, with these few exceptions:

Sitting in a cage at the zoo

Standing in a bikini

The "It's" Man also appeared in a Vox Pops segment on taxation, saying, "I would tax Raquel Welch. I've a feeling she'd tax me."

Third Series

Aside from his close-up introductions, "It's" Man appearances in the third series featured him as follows:
In a boxing ring
Saying "Lemon Curry"
Hosting his own TV show, entitled "It's," featuring Lulu and Ringo Starr

Fourth Series

The only appearance by the "It's" Man is a quick shot of him in the boxing ring saying "It's" just prior to the opening titles in the "Anything Goes/The Light Entertainment War" show.

The Arthur and Ken Quiz

Yes, of all the character names in *Monty Python's Flying Circus,* the two used most often were Arthur and Ken. Like much of Python, there seems to be no logical reason for this. John Cleese and Graham Chapman have laid the blame on Michael Palin and Terry Jones for Ken; they claim that Palin and Jones went through a stage where the pair would call everything Ken. Chapman himself was fond of the name Arthur, a fact that he attributed to British comedian Arthur Lowe.

At any rate, several names were used quite often in the shows, including Ron and Brian—even the name Bevis was used more than once. But none were used more often than Arthur and Ken.

The challenge here is to identify the characters listed or described below. Each of them is named either Arthur or Ken; the tricky bit is to separate them from each other.

1. Mr. Buddha and his inflatable knees
2. Mr. Name by name but not by nature

3. The host of "It's a Tree"
4. Biggles, partnered with Algy
5. Mr. Dove, interested in shouting
6. Mr. Shabby, the future bridegroom
7. Flight Lieutenant Frankenstein (Mrs.), letter writer
8. Mr. Lust, the Compere
9. The Wilson "twins," who sign up to go mountaineering
10. Mr. Figgis, actor and presenter of "It's the Arts"
11. The late Mr. Aldridge, a witness
12. The timid Mr. Putey
13. Mr. Frampton, the man with three buttocks
14. Mr. Ewing and his musical mice
15. The coal-mining son of a playwright
16. Mr. Jackson, who dresses up like mice
17. Mr. Waring, emcee of "The Epilogue"
18. Mr. Lemming of the British Dental Association
19. Brigadier Gormanstrop (Mrs.), prolific letter writer
20. A nonillegal robber
21. Mr. Clean-Air Systems, the boxer
22. Rev. Belling of St. Loony
23. Mr. X, sheep, leader of the Pennine Gang
24. Mr. Andrews of "How Not to Be Seen"
25. Mr. Crackpot of Crackpot Religions
26. Reginald Webster and Norman Potter, murder victims
27. Mr. Russell, director of "Gardening Club"
28. Mr. Ludlow Memorial Baths, site of "The All-England Summarize Proust Competiton"
29. Mr. Verybigliar, advantages of building by hypnosis
30. Brigadier Farquar-Smith of the British Well-Basically Club
31. Professor Rosewall, penguin researcher
32. Mr. Mee of the "Summarize Proust Competition"
33. Mr. Huntingdon of "Tenant of Wildfell Hall"
34. Mr. Huddinut, mayor of North Malden
35. Mr. Hotchkiss, author of "Devonshire Country Churches"
36. The mounted policeman from "Gay Boys in Bondage"
37. Inspector Perry, friend of Inspector Gaskell
38. Sir Clark, who fights Jack Bodell
39. Mr. Briggs, Showbiz Award winner
40. Mr. S.C.U.M.
41. Mr. Entrail, Mrs. Entrail's youngest son, neighbors of Mr. Neutron

69

42. Lord Tenniscourt, who recites "The Charge of the Ant Brigade"

Bonus Film Questions: (a) In *Meaning of Life,* who was Mr. Jarrett, whose chosen method of death was to be chased by a mob of naked ladies carrying cricket bats? (b) Who was the King who sought the Holy Grail?

The Fab Four

Monty Python fans are very often Beatles fans and vice versa. There are a number of similarities between the two groups, and more than once, Python has been called the "Beatles of comedy."

In fact, the members of each group have admired the work of each other, and some have participated in the others' projects. Of course, the best example of this would be the Rutles, Eric Idle's tribute/parody. Shot as a ninety-minute special for Lorne Michaels and NBC-TV in America, the pseudodocumentary *The Rutles: All You Need Is Cash* is the story of four lads from Rutland whose legend will last a lunchtime. An array of guest stars from Python and the *Saturday Night Live* cast brought Idle's script to life, tracing the history of the pre-Fab Four. Music was furnished by Neil Innes, whose original songs were uncanny recreations of the Beatles sound (His John Lennon-ish "Cheese and Onions" has been erroneously included on Beatles bootlegs; his "Get Up and Go" was not allowed on the original soundtrack album because it was allegedly too similar to "Get Back").

Following are a few of the connections among the members of both groups.

George Harrison has the closest ties to the Pythons, and Python fans owe him a great deal. When EMI backed out of financing *Life of Brian,* George stepped in and raised the money; as a fan, he said he simply wanted to see the film. As a result of its success, he became involved in the movie business—the creation of his Handmade Films is a direct result of *Brian,* and he even made a brief, one-word cameo appearance in the movie.

Harrison has been quoted as saying that *Monty Python* is what helped him get over the breakup of the Beatles. He first met Eric Idle when the latter had traveled to Los Angeles to promote *Monty Python and the Holy Grail,* and the two became longtime friends. Idle directed the promotional films for his "Crackerbox Palace" and "True Love" songs (in the days before MTV); Harrison included "The Lumberjack Song" on a tape of incidental music played just prior to beginning his 1974 concert dates. Harrison made a brief guest appearance on Idle's *Rutland Weekend Television* doing "The Pirate Song" (which he cowrote with Idle) and even played a TV reporter in *The Rutles,* interviewing Michael Palin (who played the Allen Klein figure). Idle also provided a guest vocal on Harrison's "This Song" single and wrote the liner notes for *The Traveling Wilburys, Volume Three,* while Palin wrote the liner notes for *The Traveling Wilburys, Volume One.*

Harrison also served as executive producer for several of the individual Pythons' films made for Handmade, including *Time Bandits, Privates on Parade,* and *The Missionary.* George wrote "Dream Away," the song that appears over the closing titles of *Time Bandits.* And he even wrote the introduction to *The First 200 Years of Monty Python.*

Ringo Starr has the distinction of being the only Beatle to appear on the Python TV series. Following the credits at the end of series 3, show 2, the "It's" Man appears to host a talk show entitled, appropriately, "It's" (as soon as he says the name of the show, the titles begin rolling). His two guests are Ringo and Lulu, although they actually have very little to do.

Michael Palin says that while writing the sketch, they wanted "two extraordinarily famous people," and they were thinking along the lines of John Lennon and Yoko Ono. But it turned out that Ringo was a friend of Graham Chapman's, and the drummer proved to be quite happy to participate.

Ringo had actually met Chapman and John Cleese a few years earlier, when he was costarring with Peter Sellers in *The Magic Christian*. Graham and John both did some writing and acting for the film (Graham as part of a rowing team, John in an auction scene), and Graham and Ringo shared mutual friends like Harry Nilsson and Keith Moon—so Ringo (briefly) joined the *Flying Circus*.

Paul McCartney's Python connections are a bit more tenuous, although he is certainly a fan: In a 1989 *Rolling Stone* cover story, McCartney described how he and wife Linda would often do Python lines and voices with each other.

There was another Python brush with McCartney in the early 1970s, however. McCartney (who had, incidentally, composed some music for the aforementioned *Magic Christian*) hosted a party at the London Hard Rock Cafe to introduce his new group, Wings. The compere for the evening's festivities was none other than Graham Chapman. But it didn't turn out as planned. In fact, Graham devoted a whole chapter to the incident in his *Liar's Autobiography, Volume VI*. Through no fault of his own, Graham was attacked by a large woman and her tiny escort, Cosmo—and Graham was thrown out of the club before the festivities could get under way (later, his neck became infected where Cosmo had scratched him, leading to an incident during Python filming in which, half-dressed as Mrs. Entity and half as the Colonel, he attempted to buy needles and syringes).

As far as is known, McCartney is not aware of the incident.

Finally, John Lennon admitted to being a Python fan in an interview conducted just two days before he died. Speaking at the Hit Factory with the BBC's Andy Peebles on December 6, 1980, Lennon said, "I love *Fawlty Towers*—I'd like to be in *that,* you know! I mean, part of me would sooner be a comedian, I just don't have the guts to stand up and do it. But I'd love to be in Monty Python, rather than the Beatles, in a way."

Pythons and Other Animals: The Quiz

Animals have always played a peculiar role in the saga of Monty Python in a variety of ways that would startle polite company. Whether they're robbing banks, being converted to other species, or are simply dead, animals have always been a fertile area for Python comedy.

The group managed to use all manner of fish, fowl, and furry creatures in their sketches and used them consistently throughout all four series. The challenge of the Python animal quiz is to match the animals listed with the appropriate sketch (or sketches—some animals were featured more than others) for each series.

First Series

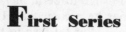

1. Pigs	a. Used in self-defense
2. Sheep	against a mob armed with
3. Mice	raspberries

4. Hippopotamus
5. Tiger
6. Rabbit
7. Cat
8. Lizard
9. Camel
10. Parrot
11. Llama
12. Goat
13. Lion
14. Terrier
15. Gorilla
16. Albatross

b. Becomes a complacent and needs to be confused

c. Converted into a fish at a pet shop

d. Sold at the cinema on an ice-cream tray

e. Apparently applies for a job as a librarian

f. Squashes animated bunnies in the titles to "Storytime"

g. Part of a discussion group, along with a duck, on customs regulations

h. Crossed off of chalkboard after being sat upon

i. Bereft of life, it rests in peace

j. It isn't well and goes on the carpet

k. Chartered accountants want to tame these

l. Trained to squeak at a selected pitch when struck by mallets

m. Flopsy, the Big Cheese's pet

n. Its numbers are on the side of the engine above the piston block

o. A quadruped that lives in large rivers like the Amazon

p. Flies across the studio and lands in a bucket of water

q. Men dress up like these in secret

r. They try to fly under the misapprehension that they're birds

Second Series

1. Cow
2. Hedgehog
3. Sheep
4. Parrots
5. Chicken
6. Mosquito
7. Mynah bird
8. Cat
9. Penguin
10. Lion
11. Fish
12. Pigeon

a. A rat catcher finds these in the wainscoting
b. Twenty-foot-high electric version with tentacles
c. Gets in a fistfight with Scott of the Antarctic
d. Teases Beethoven about going deaf
e. They destroy the Killer Cars
f. With ravenous appetites, they allegedly eat sausages, etc.
g. Vicious gang led by Eggs Diamond
h. They announce TV programs and present them for each other
i. The giant animal who watched Dinsdale
j. Hunted by Hank and Roy Spim; most dangerous when wounded
k. Explodes when on the telly
l. People who fancy them are raced in Trafalgar Square
m. Analyzed on a psychiatrist's couch

Third Series

1. Cat
2. Budgie
3. Fish
4. Rat
5. Pantomime Horse
6. Brontosaurus
7. Mollusks
8. Shark
9. Pantomime Goose
10. Penguins

a. Object of a theory by Anne Elk
b. Engage in life-or-death struggle over corporate job
c. John uses a large one to knock Michael into a canal
d. Attacks residents at 22A Runcorn Avenue
e. Intelligence proved equal to non-English-speaking persons
f. On British Showbiz Awards panel
g. Found in the cake, sorbet, pudding, and strawberry tart
h. They breed in the sewers
i. Perform on horseback in the "Ideal Loon Exhibition"
j. Takes four hours to bury
k. It's sex life is the object of a documentary

Fourth Series

1. Ant	a.　Given drugs by Mrs. Quinn
2. Sperm whale	b.　Disguise used by Teddy Salad
3. Dog	c.　Set into a wall and used as a doorbell
4. Cat	d.　Used as a garage by Mr. Quinn
5. Tiger	e.　Pet that doesn't need to be fed

he Flying Circus Hit Parade: The Top 50 TV and Movie Songs

1. "The Lumberjack Song": say no more.

2. "Every Sperm Is Sacred": from *Meaning of Life,* it manages to combine irreverence, satire, social commentary, and silliness in one of the best movie musical numbers in many years.

3. "The Galaxy Song": an amazing, scientifically accurate tour of the universe, courtesy of Eric Idle.

4. "Spam": performed by a chorus of Vikings, of course.

5. "Always Look on the Bright Side of Life": a wonderful number sung by a group of crucifees that sent audiences out of theaters singing.

6. "The Money Song": sung by Eric Idle as host of "The Money Programme," with first-rate choreography.

7. "Dennis Moore" themes: the best TV show theme parody (the "Atilla the Hun Show" theme is actually the "Debbie Reynolds Show" theme, so it doesn't quite count).

8. "Eric the Half-a-Bee": the song was actually cut from the Fish License Sketch but is performed on the *Monty Python's Previous Record* album; it is one of the extremely rare John Cleese vocal performances.

9. "Ballad of Sir Robin": an ode to courage, sung by minstrel Neil Innes.

10. "Camelot": a quick tune that manages to acquaint audiences with the fabled silly land.

11. "The Meaning of Life": a wonderful theme song, accompanied by wonderful animation.

12. "Oh Lord, Please Don't Burn Us": an inspiring hymn, another rare John Cleese toe-tapper.

13. "Sergeant Duckie's Song": an often overlooked song performed by Terry Jones as part of the Eurovision song contest.

14. "Yangtse Song": actually, only the instrumental portion of the Eric Idle song is heard in the TV shows—it accompanies some Gilliam animation of two trees growing into outer space.

15. "Llama Song": short and sweet, a guitarist and his accompanists sing the Spanish lyrics.

16. "Anything Goes": by the *other* Cole Porter.

17. "When Does a Dream Begin": this Neil Innes song is the closest the Pythons ever came to a legitimate love song, and it isn't at all silly—just a very nice 1940s-style tune.

18. "Accountancy Shanty": the theme song of the Crimson Permanent Assurance.

19. "The Blue Danube": the exploding version, that is.

20. "Brian's Theme": another rousing movie theme, with rousing animation to accompany it.

21. "The Penis Song": by Noel Coward—or was it Eric Idle?

22. "Amontillado": performed by Spanish singers in praise of their favorite sherry.

23. "King George III": performed for the King by the "Ronettes" (and composed by Neil Innes).

24. "Don't Sleep in the Subway . . .": performed by Cardinal Richelieu, sounding just like Petula Clark.

25. "Only Make-believe": sung by Prof. R. J. Gumby as he hits himself on the head with bricks.

26. "Bing Tiddle Tiddle Bong": sung by Inspector Zatapathique as part of the Eurovision song contest.

27. "Conrad Poohs and His Dancing Teeth": wonderful music courtesy of Mr. Gilliam's animation.

28. "If I Were Not Before the Bar": sung by the Counsel at the trial of Harold Larch.

29. "If I Were Not in the CID": sung by Inspector Dim at the same trial.

30. "Jerusalem": performed as "And Did Those Teeth in Ancient Time" by a guitar player live from the Cardiff Rooms, Libya.

31. "La Marseillaise": performed by a man with a tape recorder up his nose (and his brother's nose).

32. "The Bells of St. Mary's": partially performed by Arthur Ewing and his musical mice.

33. "Men of Harlech": performed on bicycle bells by the Rachel Toovey Bicycle Choir.

34. "Today I Hear the Robin Sing . . .": performed by Sir Robert Eversley at an archaeological dig; John Cleese (Eversley) lip-syncs the song, which is actually sung by Terry Jones.

35. "Jack-in-a-Box": the Clodagh Rogers/Mr. Gulliver hit.

36. "My Mistake": sung by Terry Jones as an Italian waiter.

37. "Lemming of the BDA": identified in the script as "a song which Graham knows the tune of."

38. "If I Ruled the World": sung by Lenin.

39. "Old-fashioned Girl": performed by Mr. Gulliver (Terry Jones)—as Eartha Kitt—at the Russian 42nd International Clambake.

40. "Hello Operator . . .": from "Sandy Wilson's 'The Devils.'"

41. "And Did Those Feet . . .": sung to the tune of "Jerusalem" in order to get the bag off Mr. Lambert's head.

42. Poet jingle: sung to an animated commercial for the East Midlands Poet Board.

43. "She's Going to Marry Yum Yum": sung by a pilot (Michael Palin) to the family that loathes tinny words.

44. "Yummy Yummy Yummy, I've Got Love in My Tummy": by Jackie Charlton and the Tonettes in packing crates.

45. Proust summary song: an unsuccessful attempt by the Bolton Choral Society that doesn't even get as far as the first volume.

46. Tchaikovsky piano concerto: heard when the Royal Philharmonic goes to the bathroom.

47. "Vocational Guidance Counselor": an introduction to the sketch.

48. "We're All Going to the Zoo Tomorrow": an auditory hallucination heard by Mr. Notlob.

49. The Herman Rodrigues Four: a Mexican rhythm combo playing a conga in Mrs. Vera Jackson's bedroom.

50. "Tchaikovsky's First Piano Concerto in B-flat Minor": played by Sviatoslav Richter as he escapes from a sack, three padlocks, and a pair of handcuffs.

The Monty Python's Flying Circus Ridiculously Trivial Not-Quite-as-Easy-As-the-First-Section Trivia Questions

The questions in the middle bit may make you think a bit more than you had to for the ridiculously easy first section. In fact, if you're having trouble, perhaps the best thing to do is play back the shows in your brain and try to recall snippets of dialogue or peculiar visuals. Or play back the shows on your television and try to painstakingly pick up on the phrases in question. Or admit defeat and turn to the answer page.

Not-Quite-as-Easy First Series Questions

1. Who wrote the funniest joke in the world?
2. How do you make a Nazi Cross?
3. What is the most dangerous of animals?
4. Why was Cardinal Richelieu called to testify for Harold Larch?
5. What is Charles Fatless's secret?
6. What planet and galaxy do the blancmanges come from?

7. How much money did Wilkins (the new chartered accountant) embezzle?
8. According to Mr. Verity, how much is his store's cheapest bed?
9. What do the Hell's Grannies blow their money on?
10. Where did the barber spend "five ghastly years?"
11. Where did Victor and Iris work?
12. What food does Audrey Equator ask for?
13. What are Mr. Anchovy's qualifications to be a lion tamer?
14. Where is Ron Obvious from?
15. Who managed Ron Obvious when he attempted the cross-Channel jump?
16. Where is Luigi Vercotti from?
17. What is Jimmy Buzzard opening?
18. What does Ken Shabby's grandmother do for a living?

Not-Quite-As-Easy Second Series Questions

1. What is the name of the Anglo-French Silly Walk?
2. Who expects the Spanish Inquisition?
3. What did Dinsdale Piranha do to Mrs. Stig O'Tracy?
4. Who participates in the discussion on censorship with Derek Hart and the Bishop of Woolwich?
5. What does the program "It's the Mind" examine?
6. Which fishy after-shave does the chemist go downstairs to find?
7. The subject of "Blackmail"'s Stop the Film segment belongs to what organization?
8. What musical does Mr. Praline play the piano for?
9. What does the Book-of-the-Month Club give away with every third book?
10. How is Raymond Luxury-Yacht pronounced?
11. What is the rate of interest on a piece of moss or a dead vole?
12. What animal does the rat catcher find in Mr. and Mrs. Concrete's wainscoting?
13. What is rule six?
14. Which church is Rev. Arthur Belling the vicar of?
15. What time does the penguin on top of the telly explode?

16. Who is winning in the football match between the Bournemouth Gynecologists and the Long John Silver Impersonators?
17. What is the name of Mr. Praline's pet fish?
18. Coventry City last won the FA Cup in what year?
19. What is the first lesson of not being seen?
20. Which sketch did the queen tune in to the show to see?
21. Who was the lady fired from the torpedo tube?

Not-Quite-as-Easy Third Series Questions

1. Who are the guest stars on "It's"?
2. Which community provided information for the exciting Icelandic saga?
3. Who flushed her budgie down the loo?
4. What developing market is the firm of Slater Nazi looking to expand into?
5. Who presents the *Flying Circus* show following the Anagrams Sketch?
6. What effect does Mr. Horton have on his co-workers?
7. Who is awarded first prize in the "Summarize Proust Competition"?
8. What happens to the house condemned by the Househunters?
9. Which is the randiest of the gastropods?
10. What is the first item on the menu of international cuisine?
11. Why is there no Camembert in the cheese shop (even if it's runny)?
12. Where does Ronald Rodgers of "Storage Jars" report from?
13. Why does Mr. Pither ask a doctor for directions?
14. Who does Mr. Gulliver—as Eartha Kitt—transform into next?
15. What do the three guests have in common on "Is There?"
16. Who is the housing development in Bristol being built by?
17. What film takes place in Syria, 1203?
18. On standard IQ tests, penguins score worse than Kalahari bushmen but better than what other group?
19. Who hosts "The British Showbiz Awards"?
20. The Mountbatten Trophy, show business's highest accolade, was won by whom?

Not-Quite-As-Easy Fourth Series Questions

1. Who is the cleaner of the Montgolfier brothers?
2. Who enters the King's chambers to sing "King George III"?
3. What is the advantage of owning an ant as a present?
4. Which of Chris Quinn's pets is his father using as a garage?
5. What does the young airman sing to the WAAF after World War II enters a sentimental stage?
6. Who was the winner of the Queen Victoria Handicap?
7. Where is Teddy Salad hiding?
8. Who is the most dangerous and terrifying man in the world?
9. What does Mrs. Garibaldi iron on "The Most Awful Family in Britain"?

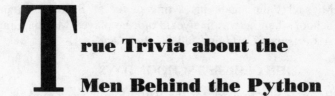

True Trivia about the Men Behind the Python

WHAT'S IN A NAME

John Cleese's real family name was Cheese—his grandfather changed it long before his grandson could write a sketch about a shop that sold it.

John also wrote for a time under the name John Otto Cleese, although his real middle name is Marwood.

MAD ABOUT TERRY

One of Terry Gilliam's first jobs upon graduation from college was assisting Harvey Kurtzman in editing *Help!* magazine in the mid-1960s. Gilliam later named one of the bureaucrats (played by Ian Holm) in *Brazil* after Kurtzman (who created *Mad* magazine and co-created "Little Annie Fanny" for *Playboy*).

Prior to Gilliam, Kurtzman employed an assistant who went on to create her own magazine—a woman named Gloria Steinem.

IDLE CHATTER

One of Eric Idle's first jobs for the BBC was working for David Frost, for whom he was hired to write "clever ad-libs."

GREAT EXPECTATIONS

Michael Palin made his acting debut at Birkdale Preparatory School when he was five years old; he played Martha Cratchit in *A Christmas Carol* and fell off the stage.

JOHN CLEESE'S SCHOOL DAYS

Before going to work for the BBC, John Cleese read for the bar at Cambridge and had intended to become a barrister. He also spent two years at another career which is not as well known—he worked as a schoolteacher, instructing ten year olds.

STRANGE BREW

With money he made from *Monty Python and the Holy Grail,* Terry Jones invested in a small brewery in the English country-side; the Penrhos Brewery specialized in real ale. Terry also became active in CAMRA, the Campaign for Real Ale, a group that supported noncarbonated, nonpressurized brews made without preservatives—completely natural beer.

MORE NAME STRANGENESS

Terry Gilliam's middle name is actually Vance, a fact that the other Pythons have utilized in somewhat silly ways. This is the reason that, during the lecture on humor seen in *Monty Python Live at the Hollywood Bowl,* when Palin, Jones, and Gilliam are demonstrating slapstick bits, Michael gets Terry's attention at one moment by calling out, "Hey, Vance!"

TV TRIVIA

The only Python to star in his own American network situation comedy is Eric Idle; he was featured in NBC's short-lived *Nearly Departed* from April 10th to May 1st, 1989.

There were two guest appearances on American sitcoms that featured Pythons, however. Idle appeared on *Laverne and Shirley* (for friend Penny Marshall) in 1981, and John Cleese won an Emmy Award for his appearance on *Cheers* on March 5, 1987.

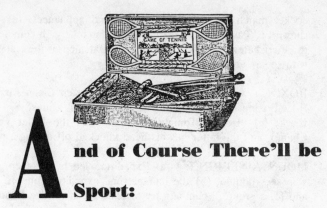

And of Course There'll be Sport:

The Sporting Events of

Monty Python

1. SOCCER/FOOTBALL: (a) A football match is played by one man, because everyone else has been turned into Scotsmen by the blancmanges; (b) an interview with footballer Jimmy Buzzard; (c) a football match with the Bournemouth Gynecologists against the Watford Long John Silver Impersonators; (d) "World Forum" asks Karl Marx, Lenin, Mao Tse-tung, and Che Guevara questions about football; (e) Football commentary is heard on the radio in the background as the Garibaldi family vies for the "Most Awful Family in Britain" title; and (f) a rugby match is played with the boys team taking on the schoolmasters in *Meaning of Life*. *NOTE:* One of the two German shows features a football match between Greek and German philosophers, also included in *Monty Python Live at the Hollywood Bowl*.

2. CRICKET: (a) "All-in cricket" is presented on "Interesting People" as two cricketers pummel each other with bats; (b) a professional cricketer appears briefly on "Spectrum"; (c) six cricketers enter a middle-class flat searching for the third test against the West Indies and encounter a rat catcher; (d) three commentators watch a

cricket match played with furniture and appliances; (e) clips are shown of "Pasolini's 'The Third Test Match,'" with commentary by three cricketers; and (f) the legendary Batsmen of the Kalahari play with spears and machetes.

3. BOXING: (a) A documentary on boxer Ken Clean-Air Systems; (b) "Boxing Tonight" features Jack Bodell against Sir Kenneth Clark; (c) "Boxing Tonight" also features the Killer versus the Champ, and the latter has his head knocked off during a match.

4. MOUNTAINEERING: (a) Expedition led by Sir George Head, who sees double; (b) the hairdressers' expedition on Mt. Everest; and (c) a group of climbers try to scale the Uxbridge Road.

5. RACING: (a) Furniture and other appliances race at Epsom; (b) a jockey is interviewed, with Queen Victoria winning and the Queen Victoria Handicap is run at Epsom.

6. BROAD JUMP: (a) Ron Obvious attempts a cross-Channel jump; (b) film is shown of Mary Bignall's winning jump at the 1964 Rome Olympics.

7. HUNTING: (a) Film of a hunting expedition in which the participants fire wildly at random; (b) Hank and Roy Spim hunt mosquitoes, moths, and ants.

8. TENNIS: Angus Podgorny plays a blancmange at Wimbledon.

9. WRESTLING: On "The Epilogue," a monsignor and a humanist tussle to determine the existence of God.

10. AUTO RACING: Formula Two car racing underwater.

11. SHOW JUMPING: The horses leap over the casts of "Oklahoma!" and "The Sound of Music."

12. CROSS-COUNTRY RUNNING: Performed by hospital patients involved in Active Recuperation Techniques.

13. CABER TOSS: Performed three men to a caber, due to overcrowding caused by the blancmanges.

14. HIDE-AND-SEEK: The second leg of the Olympic final, with England versus Paraguay.

15. WIFE SWAPPING: A full card of events from Redcar.

16. ATLANTIC CROSSING: The first man to cross the Atlantic on a tricycle.

Stocking the Cheese Shop

The Cheese Shop Sketch was one of John Cleese's favorite sketches, and he claims that it was one of only two truly original sketches (the other was the Dennis Moore Sketch) that he wrote for the third series. It's one of the classic Chapman-Cleese thesaurus sketches; in fact, it mainly consists of a customer reading off a list of cheeses.

John Cleese also uses "Cheese Shop" to point out one of Graham Chapman's greatest gifts—the virtually unfailing ability to know when something is funny, an invaluable talent for two writers who have been working by themselves for hours, attempting to create comedy. And "Cheese Shop" would probably not exist if not for Graham.

During the course of writing the sketch, Cleese says he had to stop several times and ask Graham, "Is this funny?" His partner would sit back, take a puff on his pipe, and say, "Of course it is, very funny," and they would continue writing.

Below is a lengthy list of cheeses. Although none of them may be available at Mr. Wensleydale's Ye Olde Cheese Emporium, which of the following were *not* requested in the Cheese Shop Sketch?

Red Leicester	Tilsit
Caerphilly	Bel Paese
Red Windsor	Stilton
Gruyère	Norwegian Jarlsberger
Liptauer	Lancashire
White Stilton	Danish Bleu
Double Gloucester	Cheshire
Dorset Blue Vinney	Brie
Roquefort	Pont-l'Eveque
Port Salut	Savoyard
Saint-Paulin	Carre-de-L'Est
Boursin	Bresse-Bleue
Perle de Champagne	Camembert
Gouda	Edam
Caithness	Smoked Austrian
Sage Derby	Wensleydale
Gorgonzola	Parmesan
Mozzarella	Pippo Creme
Danish Fimboe	Czechoslovakian Sheep's
Venezuelan Beaver Cheese	Milk Cheese
Ilchester	Cheddar
	Limburger

Real Life

In addition to the various stock film clips and photos, the Pythons recruited a number of real-life celebrities to play themselves.

Probably the best-known appeared during the third series on a talk show called "It's," starring the "It's" Man. Ringo Starr and Lulu both appear at the beginning of the program, which ends before it can get under way.

Monty Python's Flying Circus became a favorite of TV newsreaders, though not necessarily BBC newsreaders. The largest number of real-life appearances on the show were by newsreaders, however, and served to make some of the Python sketches particularly effective. They include

—Reg Bosanquet of *The News at Ten* is reading the news when the queen switches channels from Python; he introduces the hospital using Active Recuperation Techniques.

—Richard Baker of the BBC's *Nine O'Clock News* uses

strange gestures while inappropriate photos appear behind him; his voice is drowned out by "BBC announcers." He finally ends by speaking in anagrams. He also makes an appearance later in the series doing a story on "Storage Jars" as well as a drop-in asking, "Lemon Curry?"

—David Hamilton of Thames TV appears at the beginning of Show #39, promising an action-packed evening on Thames while presenting a "rotten old BBC program."

—ITV's Peter Woods appears in the fourth series to report that the Second World War has entered a sentimental stage.

In addition to newsreaders and singers, a sports figure made a brief appearance in the fourth series. Jimmy Hill appears dressed as Queen Victoria as he analyzes the European Cup.

The Pythons used the real names, if not the actual crew members, in a couple of instances. TV series editor Ray Millichope's name was used on two occasions. In Show #19, a "Ray Millichope, leader of the Allied Technician's Union," helps form a human pyramid in the TV studio; in Show #37, a "Mr. Millichope" is shown lying in a hospital bed in which a doctor is removing the money from patients. Also, crew member Roger Last's name was used on Show #36 as the host of "Is There?," a talk show discussing life after death.

Several Python relatives appeared in the TV series and related projects. Most prominent of those is Connie Booth, John Cleese's first wife, who cowrote and costarred in *Fawlty Towers,* in addition to appearing on the Python TV show. Eric Idle's first wife appeared in a few TV shows as well.

And Graham Chapman's foster son, John Tomiczek, appeared as one of the two French children who want Clodagh Rogers's autograph in "Cycling Tour." The father-daughter appearances came after Python, however—Terry Jones's daughter, Sally, played an extra in *Erik the Viking,* and John Cleese's daughter, Cynthia, portrayed his onscreen daughter in *A Fish Called Wanda.*

Python Fun And Game Shows

The Pythons always knew the value of playing, as evidenced by the quantity and variety of games they played. In addition to the many sports and athletic events featured on *Monty Python's Flying Circus,* the series also featured several other competitions and game shows. Below are listed the shows and events made famous on the series—the object is to match the competitions with the goals of their contestants.

1. "It's Wolfgang Amadeus Mozart"
2. "Blackmail"
3. "Beat the Clock"
4. "Historical Impersonations"
5. "Prejudice"
6. "The Most Awful Family in Britain"
7. "The All-England Summarize Proust Competition"
8. "World Forum"
9. "Spot the Loony"
10. "Ideal Loon Exhibition"

11. "Upper-Class Twit of the Year"
12. "It's a Living"
13. "Spot the Brain Cell"

a. Contestants and callers attempt to demean minorities of all kinds
b. The competitors answer a variety of questions on British football and other subjects
c. Contestants try to send in money before their identities are revealed
d. Contestants receive a large fee, three drinks at the BBC, an additional fee, a surprise, and a special fee
e. Historical characters and others attempt to die in the most spectacular manner
f. The winning contestant received the blow on the head
g. Contestants unscramble letters to spell "merchant bank "
h. Characters from history present their impressions of famous persons and incidents
i. Numbskulls and boobies from all over the country go through their paces, climaxed by the judging
j. Events include kicking the beggar, taking the bra off the debutante, and the matchbox jump
k. Competitors attempt to score highest with the judges on the disgustometer
l. Each contestant has fifteen seconds to give a brief summary of *A la Recherche du Temps Perdu*
m. The panel has to identify the loony after seeing pictures of all kinds of people in all kinds of places

The Python 500: The Top 30 Companies and Services

1. THE MULTIMILLION POUND CORPORATION: After making a complete annual profit of one shilling, their accountant is fired for embezzling a penny.

2. THE VERY BIG CORPORATION OF AMERICA/THE PERMANENT ASSURANCE COMPANY: The former was actually overrun by the latter in a hostile takeover, which occurred when the insurance pirates boarded the corporation's headquarters in *Meaning of Life.*

3. SLATER NAZI: Keen to get into the developing market of orphans, one of their merchant bankers is unable to comprehend the concept of a "gift."

4. IRVING C. SALTZBERG PRODUCTIONS: Run by a very rich film producer who needs a labotomy and can't stand yes-men.

5. CRACKPOT RELIGIONS, LTD.:   The first religion with free gifts, run by Arthur Crackpot (President and God).

6. AMERICAN DEFENSE: Nine out of ten small countries choose American defense.

7. LIFE INSURANCE, LTD.: Requires that people wanting life insurance fill up a twelve-gallon churn with ummm, to prove they're serious about wanting insurance.

8. "NO TIME TO LOSE" ADVICE CENTRE: Assists people in using the phrase in everyday conversation.

9. THE LEAGUE FOR FIGHTING CHARTERED ACCOUNTANCY: Helps to combat this terrible debilitating social disease.

10. ROYAL SOCIETY FOR PUTTING THINGS ON TOP OF OTHER THINGS: A meaningless body of men that gathers together for no good purpose.

11. THE VERRIFAST PLANE COMPANY: Their pilot is the very nice Mr. Kamikaze.

12. THE CHIPPENHAM BRICK COMPANY: Sponsor of Ron Obvious on his cross-Channel jump, they pay all his bills, and Ron carries half-a-hundredweight of their bricks.

13. CONFUSE-A-CAT, LTD.: Europe's leading cat-confusing service.

14. INTERESTING LIVES—"PURCHASE A PAST": An animated company that specializes in selling bits from other people's lives to pretend are from your life.

15. THE BBC: A bit low on money; must recruit people to appear in sketches. Their program planners are not quite as intelligent as penguins.

16. PSYCHIATRIST'S DAIRY, LTD.: Door-to-door psychiatry.

17. MINISTRY OF SILLY WALKS: Research and development; however, the government is currently spending less on Silly Walks than it is on National Defense.

18. ACME TOILETS: As seen in an animated commercial, they are endorsed by the Royal Philharmonic.

19. ROYAL HOSPITAL FOR OVERACTING: Includes Long John Silvers, King Rats, and (worst of all) the Richard III ward.

20. NORTH MALDEN ICELANDIC SAGA SOCIETY: Aimed at welcoming businessmen and investors to North Malden.

21. COLIN MOZART'S RODENT EXTERMINATION BOUTIQUE: Rats exterminated, mice punished, voles torn apart by Munich's leading furry-animal liquidator.

22. ST. POOVES HOSPITAL: Employs Active Recuperation Techniques. *ALSO:* ST. NATHAN'S HOSPITAL FOR YOUNG ATTRACTIVE GIRLS WHO AREN'T PARTICULARLY ILL, and ST. GANDALF'S HOSPITAL FOR VERY RICH PEOPLE WHO LIKE GIVING DOCTORS LOTS OF MONEY.

23. CHARLES FATLESS: With his secret of Dynamo Tension!

24. EAST MIDLANDS POET BOARD: A poet is essential for complete home comfort and all-year-round reliability at a low cost.

25. SECURICOR AMBULANCES, LTD.:   An animated Securicor Ambulance/Armored Car burgles houses and robs pedestrians after hitting them.

26. UNEXPLODED SCOTSMAN DISPOSAL SQUAD: Russian company that handles such sensitive matters.

27. SOHO MOTORS AND THE LA GONDOLA RESTAURANT: Supplying the very best models and famous Sicilian delicacies.

28. SHRILL PETROL: Engine deposits are pushed off the face of the earth by the superior forces available to Shrill.

29. BICYCLE PUMP CENTRE: Specialists in shorter bicycle pumps.

30. YE OLDE CHEESE EMPORIUM: Run by Henry Wensleydale, shop licensed for public dancing. Finest—and cleanest—cheese shop in the district.

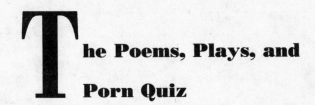

The Poems, Plays, and Porn Quiz

Monty Python always presented a variety of the arts, including poetry, drama, and literature. Listed below are the titles of some of these works; put them into the correct categories, which are also below.

1. "The Twelve Caesars"
2. "Bridget—Queen of the Whip"
3. "My new checkbook hasn't arrived"
4. "Bum Biters"
5. "Lend us a quid until the end of the week"
6. "Sister Teresa—the Spanking Nun"
7. "Can I have fifty pounds to mend the shed?"

a. Poems by Ewan McTeagle
b. Dental Plays by Martin Curry
c. Tudor Pornography

8. "Trafalgar"
9. "Gay Boys in
   Bondage"
10. "What's twenty quid
    to the bloody Midland
    Bank?"

Amazing Activities

The Python shows were filled with people performing a variety of strange and peculiar feats. The unusual activities listed below were featured in the sketches to the right. The object here is to match up the attempted feats with the sketches where they appeared.

1. Giving a cat influenza
2. Eating an Anglican cathedral
3. Becoming a gynecologist
4. Running to Mercury
5. Playing the flute
6. Jumping the English Channel
7. Sending bricks to sleep by hypnosis

a. Feats by Ron Obvious
b. On *Interesting People*
c. *How to Do It* activities
d. Ideal Loon Exhibition

8. Standing behind a
   screen with a lady
   with no clothes on
9. Splitting a railway
   carriage with the nose
10. Hanging over a tin of
    condemned veal
11. Counter-marching by
    the Massed Pipes and
    Toilet Requisites Club
12. Ridding the world of
    all known diseases

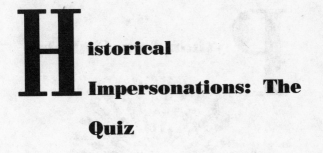Historical Impersonations: The Quiz

The ever-popular *Historical Impersonations* TV show, where "you in the present can make those in the past stars of the future," featured a wide assortment of historical talent doing a variety of impressions. The object of this quiz is to match up the historical personages with the person or thing they impersonate.

1. W.G. Grace
2. Florence Nightingale
3. Ivan the Terrible
4. Cardinal Richelieu
5. Marcel Marceau
6. Julius Caesar
7. John the Baptist
8. Napoléon

a. Graham Hill
b. The R-101 disaster
c. Brian London
d. A music box
e. A man walking against the wind
f. A sales assistant in Freeman, Hardy and Willis
g. Eddie Waring
h. A man being struck about the head by a sixteen-ton weight
i. Petula Clark

Python Fan Clubbing

Although the Pythons themselves used to discourage any attempts at an official fan club, several fans and groups have organized unofficial clubs over the years. They generally publish their own newsletters, and give other fans a chance to share their enthusiasm. There are at least two organizations going at this writing; for more information, write to them at the addresses below.

IT'S Magazine 20 Shady Lane, Nashua, NH 03062	The Ministry of Silly Walks P.O. Box 241 Oceanside, NH 11572

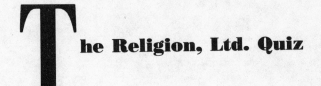

The Religion, Ltd. Quiz

The Pythons were never reluctant to take aim at religion in all its shapes and sizes, but some of their funniest moments occur when they deal with crackpot religions and their leaders. Some of the most peculiar are listed below—waiting to be matched up with the tenets of their beliefs.

1. Archbishop Nudge
2. Naughty Religion
3. Archbishop Gumby
4. Crackpot Religions, Ltd.
5. Archbishop Shabby
6. The Lunatic Religion
7. No Questions Asked Religion
8. Bishop of Dulwich

a. The first religion with free gifts
b. Believes in peace and bashing two bricks together
c. Does a lot of converting, a lot of protection

d. Raising polecats for peace
e. If you'd like a bit of love-your-neighbor
f. Likes a peace, say no more
g. Believes in the power of prayer to turn the head purple
h. Helps people help themselves—to cars, washing machines . . .

Monty Python's *Life of Brian* Quiz

1. Which of the gifts brought by the wise men does Mandy care the least about?
2. What do Brian and his mother buy just before going to the stoning?
3. What word did Matthias say that caused him to be sentenced to be stoned to death?
4. How long did the ex-leper spend "behind the bell" before he was cured?
5. Who was Nortius Maximus?
6. Which one of the revolutionaries wants to become a woman?
7. What revolutionary group does Brian join?
8. What does Brian try to paint on the wall of Pilate's palace?
9. Who does the PFJ plan to kidnap?
10. Which group do they meet beneath the palace?
11. What is the name of Pilate's very great friend who visits him from Rome?
12. What does the beard seller include when Brian haggles to buy a beard?

13. What three factions do Brian's followers split into?
14. How long did Simon the Holy Man maintain silence before Brian stepped on his foot?
15. What does the man on the cross next to Brian sing?

Movie Miscellany

Despite the Pythons tendency to dress up like women, *Monty Python and the Holy Grail* only featured one performance in drag, and that was a brief one—Terry Jones played the constitutional peasant woman out scrounging for filth.

The opening shots of the Grim Reaper dinner party scene in *Meaning of Life* are a shot-by-shot homage to Ingmar Bergman's *Seventh Seal* (as is the Grim Reaper character himself).

When the Pythons celebrated their twentieth anniversary with a party in December 1989, it was held in the same hall in London where the Mr. Creosote scenes were filmed for *Meaning of Life*.

Python Rocks!

In addition to the Beatles, a number of other rock groups share various connections with Monty Python. Below, match the rock stars with the appropriate Python association.

1. Iron Maiden
2. Mick Jagger
3. Traveling Wilburys
4. Harry Nilsson
5. .38 Special
6. Pink Floyd
7. George Harrison
8. Keith Moon
9. Sting
10. Roy Orbison

a. Interviewed by the Rutles for *All You Need Is Cash*
b. Wrote and recorded an instrumental song inspired by *Monty Python and the Holy Grail*
c. Memorized all the Python sketches
d. Album notes were written by Michael Palin and Eric Idle

e. Graham Chapman performed in a video for them

f. Made an appearance as a Mountie onstage with Python at the City Center

g. Appeared briefly in *The Adventures of Baron Munchausen* for Terry Gilliam.

h. Appeared with Eric Idle on *Rutland Weekend Television*

i. Was to appear as one of the repertory company in *Life of Brian*

j. Members helped fund *Holy Grail*

Gumby Spotting

The wonderful, handkerchief-hatted Gumbys are one of the strangest, most twisted, and funniest of Python creations. Yet one would be hard-pressed to explain to a nonfan exactly what it is that is so funny and appealing about the characters. They look quite bizarre, although their costumes are not that far removed from the way some real-life holiday makers dress at the seaside. They are incredibly dense and as stupid as comedic characters can get, although there are other Python roles just as thick (Jimmy Buzzard and Ken Clean-Air Systems come to mind).

Perhaps it's just the silliness that they apparently inspire in the Pythons themselves—the same sense of inspiration and freedom they feel when they pull on dresses and wigs to play Pepperpots—but their fans feel the same sort of exhilaration when they see the group cavorting about in boots and sweaters.

Gumbys were developed slowly, almost by accident. Michael Palin claims John Cleese threw the basic costume together for a one-line gag when they were filming on location; Palin then adapted it and gave him his "my brain hurts" persona.

The Gumbys appear in full-length sketches, in one-line Vox Pops, as links, as extras in large groups, and even in animation. Unlike many Python creations developed for the first shows, the Gumbys appeared in major sketches through the third series. All their appearances are listed below.

First Series

1. Not identified as a Gumby, John Cleese appears in a Vox Pops on customs regulations, delivering a hysterical, incoherent rant before being struck by the Knight with the rubber chicken.
2. Prof. R. J. Gumby (Graham Chapman) strikes himself on the head repeatedly with blunt instruments while crooning, "Only Make-believe."
3. Prof. R. J. Gumby (here played by Michael Palin) claims that the Battle of Trafalgar was fought on dry land near Cudworth in Yorkshire. His Gumby friend (Terry Jones) stands next to him. F. H. Gumby (Eric Idle) suggests we reappraise our concept of the Battle of Trafalgar. Prof. L. R. Gumby (Graham Chapman) agrees, and Prof. Enid Gumby (John Cleese) offers his views on cement.
4. Mr. Gumby (Terry Jones) gives his views on Hitler in a Vox Pops.
5. Two Gumbys (Terry Jones and Michael Palin) make requests for "Historical Impersonations."

Second Series

6. Mr. Gumby (John Cleese) offers his views on taxation in a Vox Pops as he stands in water.
7. A group of five Gumbys (Chapman, Cleese, Idle, Jones, and Palin) introduce the Architect Sketch and, shortly after, the Insurance Sketch. An animated "Gumby and the Beanstalk" follows later, and five animated frogs then turn into the Gumbys, who introduce the Chemist Sketch. At the end of the show, the group changes into female Gumbys, and then back again.
8. Two Gumbys (John Cleese and Michael Palin) appear in a Vox Pops to discuss their favorite after-shave lotions.

9. Archbishop Gumby (Michael Palin) talks about peace.
10. Mr. Gumby (Michael Palin) is blown up in "How Not to Be Seen."
11. Mr. D. P. Gumby (Michael Palin) stars in "Flower Arrangement."

Third Series

NOTE: Mr. Gumby does the "Monty Python's Flying Circus" voice-over during the opening titles of the third series.
12. A Gumby is part of the crowd that joins in an orgy (along with Vikings, nuns, and a Pantomime Goose) in "Ken Russell's 'Gardening Club.'"
13. T. F. Gumby (Michael Palin) appears in "Harley Street," in which he visits the Gumby Brain Specialist (John Cleese). The Gumby Surgeon (Graham Chapman) and the Gumby Anesthesiologist (Terry Jones), surrounded by five extra Gumbys, operate on him with woodworking tools.

NOTE: There were no appearances by Gumbys in the fourth series.

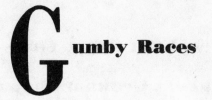Gumby Races

All of the Pythons except Terry Gilliam appeared as Gumbys throughout the series (Gilliam animated a Gumby character in the second series), but who appeared most often in the TV series with glasses, mustache, and handkerchief hat?

Counting all significant appearances, even those brief walk-ons (although the group appearances that served as links in the second series are counted as one, since they all appear together), the figures are as follows.

Michael Palin is the winner, dressing up as a Gumby eight different times; John Cleese comes in second with six appearances. He narrowly edges out Terry Jones's five and Graham Chapman's four Gumby roles, with Eric Idle's brain hurting only twice.

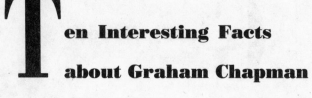

Ten Interesting Facts about Graham Chapman

1. Graham Chapman once worked as a goatherd and was always very lavish in his priase of goats as pets—he called them "very sensible animals."
2. Among other peculiar jobs, Graham Chapman once worked briefly as a writer for Petula Clark, a fact that the other Pythons delighted in reminding him of.
3. Graham was a fully qualified medical doctor; on the set of *Life of Brian* in Tunisia, he found he was devoting a large portion of his free time serving as the doctor for the film unit.
4. Although Michael Palin has kept a daily journal literally for decades, Graham is the only Python who has published (to date) his autobiography—*A Liar's Autobiography, Volume VI*.
5. Aside from Terry Gilliam's one-shot appearance on *To Tell the Truth* in 1976, Graham is the only Python to appear on an American game show, when he was part of the panel on *Hollywood Squares* for a week, around the time *Life of Brian* was opening.

6. He was indeed a fully qualified mountaineer and was used as consultant on the three Python mountaineering sketches.

7. During the 1980s, Graham embarked on a series of lecture tours that brought him to college campuses across the United States and Canada. Although they began as mostly question-and-answer sessions, the normally shy Graham developed them into full-blown lectures, interspersed with clips from Python, for the enthusiastic university crowds.

8. A portion of his money from *Monty Python and the Holy Grail* was invested in the autobiographical Muhammad Ali film, *The Greatest*.

9. After becoming involved with Britain's "Dangerous Sports Club," Graham declined an invitation to hang glide over active volcanoes in South America. Instead, he volunteered to be hurled from a huge catapult for charity and slid down a snowy hillside in a two-man boat; he escaped serious injury on both occasions.

10 At one point, Graham was writing for *three* different BBC shows at the same time (he wrote for a Ronnie Corbett TV series and *Doctor in the House* as well as for *Python*). He wrote one in the morning, one in the afternoon, and the other at night.

S *E*M*P*R*I*N*I

or

Fill in the Missing

Words

The First Series

1. The pigs go on to meet . . . . in the final.
2. Arthur Lemming attempted to buy a copy of "An Illustrated History of . . . ."
3. I'm sorry, but I don't like being called . . . . .-. . . . .
4. One thing is for sure, a . . . . . is not a creature of the air.
5. I've had more . . . . than you've had hot dinners!
6. Is you wife a . . . . ?
7. It's like . . . . . . —make a thing illegal, and it acquires a mystique.
8. Jack Riley is actually a . . . . and a cannibal.
9. Lucky we didn't say anything about the . . . .
10. It's all in a day's work for . . . . -.-. . . .
11. The palindrome of Bolton would be . . . .
12. . . . . by name not by nature.
13. Mr. Anchovy bought his lion-taming hat at . . . .

120

14. A dromedary has . . . . and a camel has a refreshment car, buffet, and ticket collector.
15. Ron Obvious has jumped nearly . . . . unofficially.
16. Terriers make lovely . . . . .
17. Keith Maniac can send . . . . . . to sleep by hypnosis.
18. The upper-class twits have to leap over . . . . levels of matchboxes.
19. Hitler and Bimmler were studying a map of . . . .
20. Somebody said . . . . to Mr. Lambert!
21. The Indian massacre at Dorking Civic Theatre is set off when . . . . fails to appear.
22. The only surviving relative of Johann Gambolputty de von Ausfern-schplenden-schlitter-crasscrenbon-fried-digger-dingle-dangle-dongle-dungle-burstein-von-knacker-thrasher-apple-banger-horowitz-ticolensic-grander-knotty-spelltinkle-grandlich-grumblemeyer-spelterwasser-kurstlich-himbleeisen-bahnwagen-gutenabend-bitte-ein-nurnburger-bratwustle-gerspurten-mitz-weimache-luber-hundsfut-gumberaber-shonendanker-kalbsfleisch-mittler-aucher von Hautkopft of Ulm is . . . . -. . . . . -. . . . . - . . . . -. . . . . - . . . . - . . . . - . . . . - . . . .

Fill in the Missing Words: The Second Series

1. Mrs. G. Pinnet is asked to sign her gas-cooker receipt with the name . . . . -. . . . . . .
2. Our chief . . . . . . is surprise, blah, blah, blah. . .
3. The secretary to the Minister of Silly Walks is Mrs. . . .-. . . . . .
4. Oh, Mr. Belpit, your . . . . are so swollen.

5. Pardon me, but I'm orf to play the . . . .
6. Are you proposing to . . . . our tenants?
7. You get a . . . . with a fully comprehensive motor in-surance.
8. Who's got a boil on his . . . . , then?
9. The BBC would like to apologize for the constant . . . . : in this show.
10. Jethro Q. Walrustitty is a member of the . . . . . party.
11. "Seven Brides for Seven Brothers" is being staged at the . . . . . . School for Boys.
12. The Grillomat Snack Bar is located in . . . .
13. Carol Cleveland is Kay Sludge, who portrays Mrs. . . . . the . . . .
14. The wings of a male . . . . can sell for up to .8 of a penny.
15. Beethoven kept a . . . . for a pet.
16. Norman St. John Polevaulter has been . . . . people for the past few years.
17. Raymond Luxury-Yacht's nose is made of . . . .
18. The cat-detector van is from the Ministry of . . . .
19. Conquistador Coffee brings a new meaning to the word . . . . . .
20. The miracle ingredient in . . . . is Fraudulin.
21. Martin has collected . . . . . . gallons of urine when he in-quires about insurance.
22. Herbert Mental collects . . . .' . . . .
23. Don't forget the Hercules Hold-em-in, the all-purpose . . . . for the man with the family hernia.
24. You don't know the difference between the Battle of Boro-dino and a . . . . .'. . . . .
25. Karl Marx played for a . . . . on "World Forum."

Fill in the Missing Words: The Third Series

1. Michael Norman Randall killed . . . . . . people on Decem-ber 19th, of 1972.
2. Arthur Huddinut is the mayor of . . . .
3. You don't want to come back from Sorrento to a . . . .

4. "A Short History of Motor Traffic Between Purley and Esher" was written by . . . .
5. Alan teaches viewers how to . . . . the . . . . . on "How to Do It."
6. An . . . . is not the same as contradiction.
7. . . . . speaks entirely in anagrams.
8. NCP Carparks has hired the . . . . to hunt down and destroy houses too dangerous to live.
9. It costs one pound for a . . . . minute argument.
10. Mount . . . . is the mountain with the biggest tits in the world.
11. Fire brigade choirs seldom sing songs about . . . .
12. . . . . is located at 22A Runcorn Avenue.
13. The most popular cheese around Wensleydale's shop is . . . .
14. After their first accident, Mr. Gulliver transforms into . . . .
15. Mr. Badger has hidden a bomb in the . . . . of the Glasgow plane.
16. Britain's first nineteen-level motorway is being built by characters from . . . .
17. Sir Philip Sidney reads Shakespeare's . . . . in . . . . to his wife.
18. The Vicar has dry sherry on the roof and . . . . in the underground tank.
19. This is a holdup, not a . . . .
20. The Laver Institute is trying to prove the . . . . is more intelligent than the human being.
21. The wild and lawless days of the post-Impressionists are featured on ". . . . ."
22. The British Showbiz Award nominations for Best Foreign Film Director are ready by . . . .'s fridge.
23. Mr. McGough has caught . . . . . in the off-license shop.
24. Mr. Gulliver entertains at the Russian 42nd International . . . .
25. Mrs. Zambesi decides to spend thirteen and six for a Curry's . . . . . .

Fill in The Missing Words: The Fourth Series

1. Keats's filthy poem is an ode to an . . . .
2. The legendary . . . . tree of Dahomey is located (sometimes) in Africa.
3. Jacques Montgolfier put the . . . . . . on the left of the sideboard.
4. Barry was the least talented of the 14 . . . . brothers.
5. Chris Quinn's ant is named . . . . . .
6. Sapper Walters used . . . . instead of ammunition to take an enemy command post.
7. Mansfield shoots a . . . . . . nibbling at the croquet hoops.
8. When Captain Carpenter arrives in the Yukon, he first claims to be from the U.S. Government . . . .
9. The Jodrell family is the winner of the . . . . Family in Britain, 1974.
10. I like this Ano-Weet, it really . . . . me.
11. The regiment presented Walters with a pair of special . . . . for obliging the men.
12. Carol's father is building a model of the . . . . as he lays in bed between his daughter and her husband.

Oscar and Monty

Although none of the Pythons have won an American Academy Award, some of their post-Python work has been nominated. Terry Gilliam's *Brazil* and *Adventures of Baron Munchausen* were both nominated for several technical Oscars, while Gilliam himself and cowriters Charles McKeown and Tom Stoppard were nominated for best screenplay. John Cleese's *A Fish Called Wanda* saw Charles Crichton nominated for Best Director.

And as many Python fans are aware, Kevin Kline won the Academy Award for Best Supporting Actor for *Wanda,* the first Oscar presented to a Python project.

What many Python fans don't know, however, is that Michael Palin won the British equivalent of that award for his role in *Wanda;* the BFI presented him with the Best Supporting Actor award for his role as the stuttering, animal-loving Ken.

Interestingly, the same year saw an American Oscar for Best Cinematography presented to Peter Biziou for *Mississippi Burning.* Ten years earlier, Biziou was the cinematographer on *Life of Brian.*

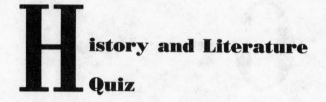

History and Literature Quiz

A number of famous figures from history and literature have made their appearances in *Monty Python's Flying Circus* in a variety of strange and silly ways. A list of them follows; the challenge is to name the person(s) listed in each series that never appeared on the Python shows.

NOTE: There may be several ringers in each series, or fewer than one.

First Series

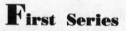

F. G. Superman	Dracula
Biggles	Ivan the Terrible
Edgar Allan Poe	King Henry VIII
Wolfgang Amadeus	Long John Silver
Mozart	Julius Caesar
Florence Nightingale	Admiral Nelson

Alexander the Great	King Arthur
Cardinal Richelieu	Marcel Marceau
Frankenstein	Genghis Khan
Napoléon	

BONUS: Which two characters above appeared in three separate sketches in the first series?

Second Series

Beethoven	Captain Ahab
Alfred Lord Tennyson	Mozart
Oliver Twist	Karl Marx
Long John Silver	Adolf Hitler
Shakespeare	Admiral Nelson
Attila the Hun	Catherine the Great
Ramsey MacDonald	Wordsworth
Richard III	Hamlet
Buzz Aldrin	Michelangelo

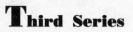

Third Series

Jean-Paul Sartre (Mrs.)	Dickens
George Bernard Shaw	Erizabeth L
Lucino Visconti	Lord of Buckingham
Sir Kenneth Clark	Sir Walter Scott
Michelangelo Antonioni	Jacques Cousteau
James McNeill Whistler	Trotsky
Oscar Wilde	Clodagh Rogers
Eartha Kitt	Dickie Attenborough
Edward Heath	Princess Margaret

BONUS: Which characters were actually played by Mr. Gulliver? Which character was actually a pantomime/dummy character?

Fourth Series

Lord North
Ferdinand von Zeppelin
Percy Shelley
Jacques Montgolfier
George III
Galileo
Prince von Bulow
Queen Victoria

Wordsworth
Keats
Hamlet
Cleopatra
Louis XIV
Churchill
Joseph Montgolfier

Skirting the Issue: Drag Races

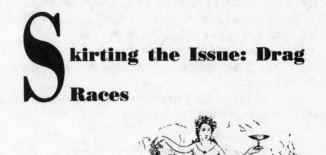

Which of the Pythons dressed in women's clothing the most often (on the TV shows, that is)?

Drag humor has long been a staple of British comedy, and the Pythons helped popularize it in America. They began playing many of the women's roles themselves because most of them were rather unflattering and far from glamorous. They felt they could play such humorous parts better than most of the real women they could have hired—or at least cheaper. Of course, the Pythons did take on Carol Cleveland and several other women for more feminine roles, but the group members themselves loved to play the older ladies (or Pepperpots, as Graham Chapman christened them).

The Pythons themselves love to joke about their penchant for dressing up like women and who actually enjoyed it the most. But who actually did appear in drag the most often in the Python TV shows?

In calculating the answer, all the significant appearances in drag were included. To complicate matters, though, is the fact that John Cleese did not appear in the six shows of the fourth series. So, through the end of the third series—including all of Cleese's appearances—the winner is Graham Chapman with thirty-six roles in drag. He is followed by Terry Jones with thirty-two, Eric Idle with twenty-four, Cleese with nineteen, while Michael Palin appeared in women's clothing only eighteen times in the first three seasons of *Python* (Terry Gilliam's single appearance in drag was in the fourth series).

The absence of Cleese in the fourth series made little difference in the final standings, however—the only change is Palin passing Cleese.

The final tallies for Python appearances in drag in the forty-five TV shows is as follows:

Graham Chapman	45 times
Terry Jones	38 times
Eric Idle	31 times
Michael Palin	26 times*
John Cleese	19 times
Terry Gilliam	1 time

The undisputed winner is, obviously, Graham Chapman!

The totals for the three original Python films are somewhat different, however. In *Holy Grail, Life of Brian,* and *Meaning of Life,* Terry Jones appeared in drag six different times (even though in *Brian* he was in drag nearly the entire film!), Eric Idle played four characters in drag (including Stan, who wants to be called Loretta), and Michael Palin portrayed only three female characters. Graham Chapman and Terry Gilliam were each only in drag one time in the films (both in *Meaning of Life*), while John Cleese never appeared in drag in the three films.

NOTE: This does not include Palin's appearance on "Historical Impersonations" as Cardinal Richelieu doing his impression of Petula Clark.

The Missing Links

In addition to the many artistic applications of Terry Gilliam's animation, it also served a more practical purpose for the other Pythons. Whenever they would have problems finding a punch line to end a sketch, they would simply abandon it in order to go on to another one. Still, they needed something to link one sketch to another.

The Pythons eventually came up with all sorts of characters (such as Mr. Gumby and the Colonel) and devices (such as different parts of the body and the Vox Pops segments) to serve as links, but perhaps the most important was the Gilliam animation. Generally given the freedom to create whatever he wanted, he wound up with some incredibly strange, funny, and surreal animation segments that helped define the Python style. And in his own inimitable manner he was able to link together sketches that the other five found unlinkable.

Listed below are sketches and animation that Terry somehow managed to link together, along with the various bits of animation that were used to link them together. The challenge is to identify the missing links above with the answers below.

1. "Confuse-a-Cat" . . . . to an animated lady packed in a suitcase and leading into the Customs Sketch.
2. Animated coffins . . . . to the "World of History."
3. A Scotsman being eaten . . . . to a cowboy's lasso becoming part of some knitting.
4. A figure in an anatomy chart . . . . to "Farming Club."
5. Communist revolutions . . . . to Putrid Peter and Barry Bigot dolls.
6. Stomping feet . . . . to opening a letter and traveling backward to the post office.
7. Heaven . . . . through a jungle to a restaurant.
8. A Queen Victoria helicopter shot down . . . . to grapes being eaten by a nude woman.
9. Reg's head being sawed off . . . . to a Civil War cannonball.
10. Animated people falling and bouncing off a nude woman . . . . to "Spectrum."
11. The giant foot crumbles . . . . to "Archaeology Today."
12. The Exchange Mart Editor . . . . to the Agatha Christie Railroad Sketch.
13. World War I planes . . . . to a nude woman in a nest that is flipped into the middle of traffic.
14. Animated rioting and an eyeball stolen . . . . to "World Forum."
15. An animated priest selling encyclopedias . . . . to "The Barber."
16. Hermits and a film crew are swept into a meat grinder . . . . to an aquarium in a pet shop with a dead parrot.

a. A magician conjures flowers and a globe
b. Botticelli's *Venus*
c. A nude policeman
d. Commercials for the Chinese Communist Conspiracy, Crelm toothpaste, and Shrill petrol
e. Character walks off the edge of the cartoon

f. Conrad Poohs and His Dancing Teeth
g. A kid floating with purple balloons
h. A garden of hands
i. Civilization arises and an elephant is reconstructed during excavation
j. An eyeball is stolen
k. Sideshow barker giving away kewpie dolls
l. A vomiting Lyndon Baines Johnson
m. *2001*-like animation
n. The general's mustache begins growing
o. A Civil War cannon shoots flying sheep
p. A bouncing Queen Victoria

Comic Book Python

The Pythons have had several encounters with the comic book industry, though most of them have been near misses. Terry Gilliam has the closest ties with the medium, growing up on Harvey Kurtzman's *Mad* in the 1950s when it was still a comic book. After his college graduation, he moved to New York to work for Kurtzman, who was then publishing *Help!* magazine. Gilliam first met John Cleese when the latter appeared in a fumetti/photo feature for *Help!* called "Christopher's Punctured Romance" (reprinted in *The First 200 Years of Monty Python*). During this time, Gilliam also had some of his own cartoons published in *Help!, Surf-toons,* and other such magazines.

Shortly after Monty Python became successful in America in the mid-1970s, Terry Gilliam met Stan Lee of Marvel Comics while visiting New York. According to Gilliam, Lee expressed enthusiasm for doing a Monty Python comic book; he apparently wanted to adapt Python TV sketches in a comic magazine. Gilliam found the idea a bit peculiar. As he expected, nothing further came of it.

Not long after, however, plans for a *Jabberwocky* comic book were announced, to be drawn by comic artist Tom Sutton. Again, nothing came of it.

A few comic strips were actually included in two other Python-related projects. In Terry Jones and Michael Palin's *Dr. Fegg's Nasty Book of Knowledge,* Frank Bellamy drew a two-page western comic strip.

And the *MONTYPYTHONSCRAPBOOK* (on the flip side of the *Life of Brian* book) includes an adaptation of the shepherd scene by noted comics artist Neal Adams, a scene that was filmed but not included in the final movie.

Another Terry Gilliam project did finally make it onto the pages of Marvel Comics. *Time Bandits* was adapted as a one-shot magazine in 1982. Sales were disappointing, but it is becoming increasingly difficult for Python collectors today to find copies in top condition.

In 1989, Chicago's Now Comics produced a four-issue adaptation of Gilliam's *Adventures of Baron Munchausen.* That same year, DC Comics expressed interest in an *Erik the Viking* comic book, but when the release date was going to be moved forward, it became impossible. Still, an oversized graphic novel adaptation of the Terry Jones film was published in Great Britain by Robson Books, illustrated by Graham Thompson, in conjunction with the release of the movie.

Terry Gilliam has also been associated with another off-again, on-again project. When producer Joel Silver first acquired the film rights to the acclaimed DC Comics series *Watchmen,* he announced that Gilliam had agreed to direct it. Rights for the film bounced around from Warner Brothers to 20th-Century Fox, and Gilliam's association with the project came and went at various times. He and collaborator Charles McKeown even took a crack at some script revisions at one point. At this writing, however, Gilliam's involvement with *Watchmen,* and indeed, the fate of the film itself, appears unlikely.

Python references still pop up in American comics today, as many of the creators are hard-core fans. An occasional character in DC's popular *Justice League* (who was in charge of their London office) is suspiciously similar to Basil Fawlty and is even assisted by his own version of Manuel; one issue even featured the character as a superhero called "The Beefeater." Variations of Cleese and/or Fawlty have even turned up in the panels of the *Dick Tracy* comic strip (usually as a shady or villainous character), thanks to writer Max Allan Collins.

The Ridiculously Trivial Monty Python's Flying Circus Brain Hurters: For Python Experts Only

Gumbys, go away, and twits, take off! This section of the quiz is for hard-core fans only, the people who have long since driven their loved ones crazy with constant repetition of Python dialogue and have worn out their welcome at dinner parties by insisting on demonstrating Gumby flower arranging.

If you're still here, take a deep breath and silly walk right on in to the ultimate Python trivia test!

Brain Hurters: The First Series

1. Who is recruited to chant laments while the Killer Joke is being defused?
2. How does Arthur Figgis know that Arthur Frampton has three buttocks?
3. What isn't as bad as spitting?
4. How many musical mice were trained by Arthur Ewing?
5. What is the name of the pet owned by the Big Cheese?
6. How is the word *splunge* defined?

7. Following the Indian massacre at Dorking Civic Theatre, who are the police anxious to speak to?
8. How many kilts did the blancmanges order from Angus Podgorny?
9. Where is a camel's number located?
10. Who are the guides for the mountaineering expedition led by Sir George Head?
11. Where are the Hell's Grannies based?
12. What magazine is David Unction caught reading?
13. Why does Mr. Gumby maintain the Battle of Trafalgar was fought near Cudworth?
14. Who won the "Upper-Class Twit of the Year" competition?
15. Which political party does Mr. Hitler belong to?
16. What are violent criminals turned into by the Special Crime Squad?
17. Who does Florence Nightingale impersonate?
18. What does the Ouija board spell out for the constables?

Brain Hurters: The Second Series

1. Who lives at 46 Egernon Road?
2. When Dinsdale was very depressed, how large was Spiny Norman?
3. What would make chartered accountancy a much more interesting job?
4. According to BALPA, how long does it take a chap to become a fully qualified airline pilot?
5. What does the airplane hijacker land on outside Basingstoke?
6. Who does the East Midlands Poet Board have in a bathtub?
7. How is Ken Clean-Air Systems currently woken up?
8. Who starred in L. F. Dibley's "Finian's Rainbow"?
9. What is the name of the killer sheep?
10. How tall is archaeology professor Robert Eversley?
11. Who lost an arm battling an ant?
12. What does Michelangelo finally decide to call his statue of David?
13. Who used the expression "Hot enough to boil a monkey's bum"?
14. Who mails a letter to the animated Conrad Poohs?

15. Why and by whom was Sir Horace killed?
16. Where is the ambiguity?
17. Who is the publisher of the English-Hungarian phrase book?
18. Where do the Vikings assemble for their Spam?
19. When was the Treaty of Utrecht ratified?
20. How many bird-watchers' eggs has Herbert Mental collected?

Brain Hurters: The Third Series

1. What is the first name of Mrs. Jean-Paul Sartre?
2. Where does the BBC live?
3. What book was Brian Norris reading in the Putney Public Library?
4. Brian Norris's real occupation is what?
5. Who started the Jungle Restaurant?
6. What was Inspector Leopard's original name?
7. Which is the right room for an argument?
8. How does Betty Bailey's expedition escape?
9. Which regiment works with fabrics and experiments with interior design?
10. How long does Mrs. Scab have to beat the clock?
11. What does Mervyn want his mother to play to keep his hamster alive?
12. Who is Biggles writing letters to?
13. What does George Jalin—the man watching the mollusk documentary—have on his back?
14. Who introduces "Mortuary Hour" on Radio Four?
15. What two activities interest the "British" in Smolensk?
16. How much is an ordinary cup of drinking chocolate on the planet Algon?
17. Which two magazines does Sir Philip Sidney seize from the Spaniards?
18. What does it say on the bag that Dennis Moore carries?
19. Which astrological sign is June 21st to June 22nd?
20. As a result of "Boxing Tonight," what does Jack Bodell become?
21. What classic is featured on the "Spot the Loony" historical adaptation?
22. To receive her new brain, what does Mrs. Zambesi have to sign?

Brain Hurters: The Fourth Series

1. What are the three advantages of voting Norwegian?
2. Why does Chris Quinn return his ant?
3. Who compiled the map of Basingstoke in Westphalia?
4. What does the presiding counsel make everyone in the room wear during Walters's court-martial?
5. What is Mr. Gabriello carrying in a bucket after the big fight?
6. How did Teddy Salad make his name?
7. What song does Giuseppe play for the Secretary of State and the Prime Minister?
8. Who has stabbed Mr. Wilkins outside his doctor's office?

Mastering The Art of Python Cooking: The Top Twenty-five Python Delicacies (in No Particular Order)

1. WHIZZO BUTTER: Nine out of ten British housewives can't tell the difference between Whizzo Butter and a dead crab.

2. Turner's *FIGHTING TEMERLAINE:*   Enjoyed by children and parents alike.

3. BANANAS, RASPBERRIES, AND OTHER FRESH FRUIT: Much more effective when used as assault weapons.

4. THE WHIZZO QUALITY ASSORTMENT: Includes Cherry Fondue, Crunchy Frog, Ram's Bladder Cup, Cockroach Cluster, Anthrax Ripple, and Spring Surprise.

5. BLANCMANGE: The outer-space variety that turns everyone into Scotsmen, in an attempt to win at Wimbledon.

6. HOPKINS AU GRATIN A LA CHEF: The special at a vegetarian restaurant, Hopkins advises customers to try him with a bit of rice.

141

7. ALBATROSS: A bloody seabird, it's not any bloody flavor.

8. LIVER AND BACON: The preferred breakfast of boxer Ken Clear-Air Systems, who places a plate of it under his chair and locks himself in the cupboard; for lunch, he crouches down in the road and rubs gravel in his hair.

9. SLICED SAMURAI: An animated segment that sees the warrior slicing everything in half, including himself, for use in a cooking demonstration.

10. ATTILA THE BUN: Animated food that attacks other animated food.

11. CABBAGE AND WEBB'S WONDER LETTUCE: Used in "Le Fromage Grand"; the latter eventually explodes.

12. CONQUISTADOR INSTANT COFFEE: "Brings a new meaning to the word *vomit*."

13. SPAM: The breakfast of Vikings. Spam, Spam, Spam, Spam . . .

14. LEG OF HODGES, CAPTAIN SOUP, ETC.:   Lifeboat cuisine for survivors who are more particular about their meals.

15. MOTHER: An appalling idea, suggested by the undertaker and his assistant and partially agreed to by her son, but much too disgusting to go into detail about . . .

16. DEAD UNJUGGED RABBIT FISH, RAT CAKE, RAT SORBET, RAT PUDDING, AND STRAWBERRY TART: Well, the strawberry tart has got *some* rat in it . . .

17. WHISKEY: Mr. Badger orders it to start with, as a main course, and for pudding, along with a bottle of wine.

18. LEMON CURRY?

19. RED LEICESTER, TILSIT, CAERPHILLY, BEL PAESE, ETC.:   Among others, varieties of cheese that are not available at Ye Olde Cheese Emporium.

20. BANANA AND CHEESE SANDWICHES: A delicacy enjoyed by Mr. Pither on his cycling tour.

21. ANO-WEET, BAKED BEANS: Favorites of the Garibaldi family, one of the Most Awful Families in Britain.

22. SIR ROBIN'S MINSTRELS: Eaten by King Arthur and his Knights during a particularly bleak winter.

23. HOWARD THE FISH: Eaten by a restaurant patron while his friends watch from a fish tank (in *Meaning of Life*).

24. ONE WAFER-THIN MINT: Tempts Mr. Creosote after an already large dinner.

25. SALMON MOUSSE: Served at a dinner party but unfortunately made with canned salmon, causing a visit by the Grim Reaper.

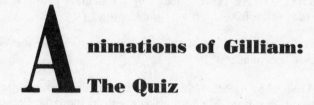

Animations of Gilliam: The Quiz

Of all the Pythons, perhaps Terry Gilliam had the most freedom to do as he pleased. For the most part, the other five would hammer out their sketches in assorted groups, then get together and compile shows out of them. However, they would leave places in the scripts where Señor Gilliam was free to insert one or two minutes of animated material—usually in places where they were unable to come up with any linking material—and they would rely on Terry to tie together two particularly troublesome sketeches.

The others would pretend to speak disparagingly of his "cartoons," although more than anything else, it was the animation that gave Python its unique look. The group realized it, although they were initially slow to acknowledge the fact. When the first two shows were done, Gilliam was not actually considered one of the team (as evidenced in the closing credits) and was paid less than the other five. It didn't take long to realize the crucial role the animation played in the stream-of-consciousness flow that the group (particularly Terry Jones) fought so hard to achieve and which set *Monty Python's Flying Circus* apart from anything else on television.

Gilliam would usually walk into the BBC studio on the day of the taping with a reel of film under his arm, often recruiting the first Python he came across to record voices for him. It is a testament to the faith they had in him that they didn't question his work but simply inserted it into the show (of course, by that time they wouldn't have been able to change it, anyway). Gilliam had usually spent several sleepless nights the previous week trying to finish the animation; he still calls it some of the hardest work he's ever done.

The fruits of his labors are on display, however, in every Python show, combining his own cartoon figures with famous works of art transformed into cutout animation. Listed below, according to series, are some of the stars of Terry Gilliam's animation work for the TV shows—the challenge is to match them with the accompanying descriptions of their role.

First Series

1. Ken Shabby	a. Becomes a musical instrument
2. Charles Fatless	
3. Long John Silver	b. Dance to jug band music
4. Royal Philharmonic	
5. Brian Islam and Brucie	c. Thought balloon deflates, as does the thinker
6. Botticelli's *Venus*	
7. Michelangelo's *David*	d. Dynamo Tension is the secret
8. Rodin's *Kiss*	
9. René Descartes	e. Falls into an aquarium at a pet shop
	f. Does ad for Acme Toilets
	g. Part of soap opera/ photo caption sequence
	h. Leaf is being pulled off
	i. Impression performed by a Chippendale writing desk

145

Second Series

1. Conrad Poohs	a. Piggy-bank hunting
2. Attila the Bun	b. Flashes sexual athletes
3. Teddy and Neddy	c. Attracts maidens with Crelm toothpaste
4. Adam (from the Sistine Chapel)	d. Discovers the Black Spot
5. Dragon	e. Possesses Dancing Teeth
6. Uncle Sam	f. Tries to sell American defense
7. Mona Lisa	g. Found wearing wolf's clothing
8. Killer Sheep	h. Slices food at the dinner table
9. The Prince	i. Becomes part of a sandwich

Third and Fourth Series

1. Toulouse-Lautrec	a. Dance to "Jack-in-the-Box"
2. Heath and Wilson	b. Appears when trees grow into outer space
3. Frog with a man's head	c. Perform "The Dance of the Sugarplum Fairies"
4. Penguins	d. Shot by slow-motion cannon
5. Maurice and Kevin	e. Stars in wild West show
6. Hitler	f. Becomes an alarm clock
7. Montgolfier Brothers	g. Take over important positions at the BBC, in government, etc.
8. The Househunters	h. Wash each other
9. Opera Singer	i. Condemn their prey and turn it into a carpark

All the Nudes That Fit

Among other ground broken (if not completely plowed under) by *Monty Python's Flying Circus* was the relatively frequent use of nudity by the Pythons themselves, assorted supporting players, and Terry Gilliam's animated segments. Each of the group members ended up participating to some degree, although none as frequently as Terry Jones, who introduced the opening titles in all but one of the shows in the third series by playing an organ fanfare while completely naked.

Aside from Terry Jones's regular appearances, who appeared nude (or nearly nude) most often in the TV shows? Intensive research exposes the following glimpses.

1. An inadvertent striptease in "Changing at the Beach," in which a man (Terry Jones) tries to change into his swimming costume. The scene is shot in a peculiar silent-movie style.
2. A naked man covering himself with a towel (Eric Idle) appears as part of the program put on by "Confuse-a-Cat, Ltd."

3. An unidentified nude woman sells a newspaper to the title character in "The Dull Life of a City Stockbroker."

4. Several animated women appear naked in the book "Full Frontal Nudity" and in the stage show that follows.

5. Two naked men (Terry Jones and Graham Chapman) appear on a talk show to discuss "Full Frontal Nudity."

6. A brief striptease (by Carol Cleveland) appears in the middle of "The World of History" as the show discusses 18th-century social legislation, with more nudity in the titles as well.

7. Hopkins (Terry Jones), the day's special at the vegetarian restaurant, is wheeled by on a serving cart; he is covered only by a bit of garnish.

8. A police car drives over a naked woman in an animated bit.

9. A nude woman (Carol Cleveland), along with several other persons, is found inside Mr. Notlob during his surgery.

10. Animation of several nude women covered with faucets, binoculars, etc., at strategic points leads into the Tax on Thingy Sketch.

11. A woman (Carol Cleveland) undresses in front of a window in a high rise as the man in the dinner jacket and his desk are hoisted up immediately outside.

12. Masonic therapy designed to turn men away from becoming masons involves using an animated nude lady for the proper response.

13. In The Insurance Sketch, a nude lady comes with every fully comprehensive motor insurance.

14. A nude man (Graham Chapman) is interviewed in a discussion on censorship.

15. "Blackmail" features the first appearance of the Nude Organist (here played by Terry Gilliam).

16. Nude animation of "sexual athletes."

17. The Secretary of State for Commonwealth Affairs (Terry Jones) does a striptease as he speaks on agricultural subsidies.

18. Village Idiot Arthur Figgis (John Cleese) is seen in bed with two very nonidiotic girls.

19. Ensign Oates (Terry Jones) takes off his clothes to use his underwear as a slingshot to kill the giant electric penguin in "Scott of the Antarctic."

20. Miss Evans (Carol Cleveland), pursued by the rolltop writing desk, has her clothing torn off by cacti also in "Scott."

21. Black-and-white film of Ramsay MacDonald (Michael Palin) stripping down to a black garter belt.
22. The Nude Organist (Gilliam again) plays chords while the prizes are shown in "Crackpot Religions."
23. An unidentified nude woman joins in orgy during "Ken Russell's 'Gardening Club.'"
24. A pair of women's breasts are exposed behind Richard Baker during *The Nine O'Clock News*.
25. Animated Page Three Girls appear following the "Judging."
26. Announcements for upcoming BBC sitcoms include "Dad's Doctor," with Terry Jones in the title role, and a topless lady running past him, followed by medical students.
27. The animated Charwoman pounds her chest until it explodes.
28. "Pasolini's 'The Third Test Match'" features his version of a cricket game, with a nude batsman (Eric Idle) and a nude couple making love as the bowler runs over them.
29. Animated Montgolfier brothers wash each other.
30. Old nude photographs are included with a summary of falling ministers and von Zeppelin.
31. A quick shot of an animated lady eating a bunch of grapes.
32. The Supreme Commander (Michael Palin) sits behind his desk and smells himself.

NOTE: Terry Jones appeared in twelve of the thirteen shows in the third series as the Nude Organist (in all but the "Cycling Tour" show) and only made a brief appearance in the fourth series. He is seen on a hillside in the country, in a warehouse, in the aftermath of an explosion, in a boxing ring, at the beach, giving an interview before his clothes fly off, and at a concert hall, where we also see an identical naked quartet.

THE TOTALS: Even without Terry Jones's (more than twelve!) appearances playing the chords on the organ, he still managed to appear naked on the TV show more than anyone else, including Carol Cleveland. The numbers are as follows.

Terry Jones: 5 times

Carol Cleveland: 4 times

Graham Chapman, Terry Gilliam, Eric Idle, Michael Palin: 2 times

John Cleese: 1 time

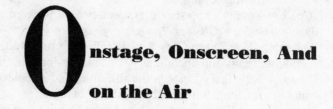

Onstage, Onscreen, And on the Air

The glittering world of show business has long been a target of the Pythons. During the flight of the *Flying Circus*, they presented a wide variety of films, TV shows, theater, and even radio, in the unique Python style.

The challenge here is to match the show with the aspect of it that the Pythons made unique. A clue—some of them may apply to more than one show. Confused? Just think of how the viewers who first saw "The Fish-Slapping Dance" must have felt . . .

The Films

1. "Wuthering Heights"	a. The Trim Jeans version (losing 1,500 inches)
2. "Rear Window"	
3. "A Tale of Two Cities"	b. The concise version, directed by L. F. Dibley
4. "Le Fromage Grand"	

5. "Gunfight at the OK Corral"
6. "Scott of the Antarctic"/"Scott of the Sahara"
7. "Ken Russell's 'Gardening Club'"
8. "Rogue Cheddar"
9. "Dr. E. Henry Thripshaw's Disease"
10. "Pasolini's 'The Third Test Match'"
11. "Ivanhoe"
12. "Sam Peckinpah's 'Salad Days'"
13. "20th-Century Frog's 'Magnificent Festering'"
14. "The Pantomime Horse Is a Secret Agent Film"
15. "The Great Escape"
16. "The Bishop"
17. "Flaming Star"
18. "Finian's Rainbow"
19. "The Black Eagle"

c. The "Spot the Loony" historical adaptation
d. Ends with a cowboy shooting a cheese vendor through the head
e. Involves cricket and people making love
f. Adapted for parrots
g. Animation of lovers making fools of themselves
h. Includes a chase with the hero and his Soviet counterpart
i. Archaeological vengeance
j. The semaphore version
k. Filmed entirely on location in Paignton
l. Set on a rubbish dump
m. Pirate film taking place in 1742
n. Blood-splattered lawn party
o. Done in Morse code
p. Set in Syria, 1203
q. Orgy with Pantomime Goose, nuns, Vikings, etc.
r. The hero and his four henchmen arrive too late

heater

1. "The Twelve Caesars"
2. "Puss in Boots"
3. "Sandy Wilson's 'The Devils'"
4. "The Moscow Praesidium Show"
5. "Othello"
6. "Gay Boys in Bondage"

a. The underwater version
b. By railroad playright Neville Shunt
c. Presented by the Redfoot tribe
d. Target of the war against porn
e. Stars Eartha Kitt and

151

7. "Hello, Dolly!"
 8. "The Reluctant
     Debutante"
 9. "The Battle of Pearl
     Harbor"
10. "Seven Brides for
     Seven Brothers"
11. "Measure for
     Measure"
12. "The First Heart
     Transplant"
13. "Dial 'M' for Murder"
14. "It All Happened on
     the 11:20 from
     Hainault to Redhill
     via Horsham, etc."

Peter Cook and Dudley
Moore
f.   By writer/dentist
Martin Curry
g.   Little-known
Shakespearean
masterpiece read by Sir
Philip Sidney
h.   Presented at a police
station in Venezuela
i.   Pawnee stole scripts of
this from the Redfoot tribe
j.   Performed by men
listening to tapes with
headphones
k.   Muddy version
performed by the Batley
Townswomen's Guild
l.   Four boys and two girls
play the lead roles

Television (and Radio)

 1. "A Book at Bedtime"
 2. "Harley Street"
 3. "Erizabeth L"
 4. "Flower
     Arrangement"
 5. "Njorl's Saga"
 6. "The Naughtiest Girl
     in School"
 7. "The Death of Mary,
     Queen of Scots"
 8. "Up Your Pavement"
 9. "The Golden Age of
     Ballooning"
10. "The British Showbiz
     Awards"
11. "Show Jumping from
     White City"
12. "No Time Toulouse"

a.   Host teaches how to
saw a lady into three bits
and dispose of the body
b.   Taught by Mr. D. P.
Gumby
c.   Obstacles include
"Oklahoma!" and "The
Sound of Music"
d.   Stars two happy-go-
lucky tramps
e.   Stars the men of the
14th Marine Commandos
f.   Series stars the
Montgolfier brothers and
their washing
g.   Family sitcom with
children Jenny and Robin
and butler Uncle Tom

13. "Conjuring Today"
14. "Hamlet"
15. "The Attila the Hun Show"

h. Tells his psychiatrist he wants to be a private dick
i. "Red Gauntlet" by Sir Walter Scott
j. A messenger on a moped arrives with news from Sir Flancis Dlake
k. Set in the wild, lawless days of the post-Impressionists
l. Icelandic adventure that takes place in Malden
m. T. F. Gumby visits the Gumby Brain Specialist
n. Hosted by a weepy Dickie Attenborough
o. Radio drama that ends with the radio exploding

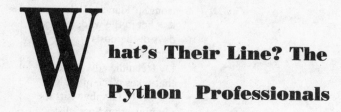

What's Their Line? The Python Professionals

Butchers, bakers, candlestick makers, and lumberjacks—the Pythons managed to play a huge variety of roles throughout the course of the TV shows. Their professions ranged from such ordinary everyday jobs as doctors and soldiers to rather specialized jobs, such as a Cardinal Richelieu impersonator.

Research into the shows reveals the professions most often portrayed by the Pythons in significant roles on TV, from the most popular to the least common. Actually, the profession most portrayed may very well be the Gas Man from the New Cooker Sketch, in which an infinitely long line of Gas Men (stretching into animation) in caps, trench coats, and glasses stand outside Mrs. Pinnet's door waiting to install her new cooker. Since most of them are simply extras and aren't played by the Pythons, they aren't included in this particular tally. So, the professions used most often in Python are listed below.

1. Policemen—51 times (by far the most-used profession)
2. Military—29 times (including two soldiers used in "Confuse-a-Cat")

3. Clergymen—28 times (including the Spanish Inquisition)
4. Doctors—27 times (interestingly, there was only one doctor used in all of the first series)
5. TV interviewers—26 times (as opposed to reporters, game show hosts, etc.)
6. Politicians—23 times
7. Shopkeepers—18 times
8. TV reporters—16 times
9. Sailors—15 times
10. Judges—14 times (including one group of six)
11. Pilots—11 times
12. Undertakers—10 times
13. (tie) Waiters, newsreaders—8 times
15. (tie) Writers, psychiatrists, and game show hosts—7 times
18. (tie) Film directors, mobsters, scientists, footballers, BBC men, village idiots, coal miners—6 times

Other Appearances

Barristers, art critics, hermits, and historians—5 times
Accountants, mountaineers, architects, insurance agents, and cricketers—4 times
Musical composers, robbers, headmasters, chemists, boxers, firemen, secret police, toupee salesmen, hairdressers/explorers—3 times
Miscellaneous civil servants, cooks, milkmen, producers, pet shop owners, nurses, waitresses, trainers, rat catchers, bank managers, archaeologists, advertising men, Richard IIIs, church police, balloonists, jockeys—2 times
And one appearance each: teacher, playwright, bicycle repairman, veterinarian, encyclopedia salesman, customs man, smuggler, stockbroker, Indian brave, camel spotter, tailor, barber, real lumberjack, would-be librarian, surgeon, mill worker, cleaner of public lavatories, flight instructor, hijacker, poet inspector, butler, Timmy Williams, skin specialist, referee, auctioneer, flower arranger, professional arguer, bus conductor, travel agent, film critic, cyclist, hypnotist, brain salesman, plumber, dentist, scrap man, trapper, conjurer, explorer, Icelandic honey salesman

The Lumberjack Song

THE BARBER: I'm a lumberjack and I'm OK,
I sleep all night and I work all day.

MOUNTIE CHORUS: He's a lumberjack and he's OK,
He sleeps all night and he works all day.

THE BARBER: I cut down trees, I eat my lunch,
I go to the lavatory.
On Wednesday I go shopping,
And have buttered scones for tea.

MOUNTIE CHORUS: He cuts down trees, he eats his lunch,
He goes to the lavatory.
On Wednesday he goes shopping,
And has buttered scones for tea.
He's a lumberjack and he's OK,
He sleeps all night and he works all day.

THE BARBER:	I cut down trees, I skip and jump, I like to press wild flowers. I put on women's clothing And hang around in bars.
MOUNTIE CHORUS:	He cuts down trees, he skips and jumps, He likes to press wild flowers. He puts on women's clothing And hangs around in bars . . . ? He's a lumberjack and he's OK, He sleeps all night and he works all day.
THE BARBER:	I cut down trees, I wear high heels, Suspenders and a bra. I wish I'd been a girlie, Just like my dear Mama.
MOUNTIES CHORUS:	He cuts down trees, he wears high heels, (spoken) Suspenders . . . and a bra? . . .

(They walk off in disgust)

GIRL:	Oh, Bevis! And I thought you were so rugged!

Words and music copyright Python Productions

157

The Monty Python's Meaning of Life Quiz

1. Why do the doctors in the birth scene ask for the most expensive machine in the whole hospital?
2. What does the Yorkshire father have to do with his children when he loses his job?
3. What is being a Protestant all about?
4. What is Carter playing with when his teacher puts on a sexual demonstration before the class?
5. What presents do the men give to their sergeant in the World War I trench?
6. How does Perkins lose his leg during the night?
7. Who guides the middle-aged American couple to the dungeon room?
8. What topic does the couple in the dungeon room choose for conversation?
9. Which organ do the doctors remove from a live donor?
10. What are the two fundamental concepts of the meaning of life, according to the man at the Very Big Corporation?
11. How does Mr. Creosote end his dinner?

12. How is Arthur Jarrett executed?
13. What food has killed the guests at the dinner party?
14. How do the guests at the dinner party travel to heaven?
15. What song does Arthur Jarrett sing in the Heaven Showroom?

Python Bloopers

One problem in trying to track down Python bloopers is identifying them. When a character changes names in the middle of a scene, is it a mistake or are they deliberately throwing viewers another curve? Or are they simply taking an embarrassing error and pretending it was intentional all along?

Actually, considering the somewhat frenzied circumstances under which the group had to record the TV shows, it's surprising there aren't a great many more fluffed lines. Once they were in the studio on Saturday night to record a show, they had only a limited time to do the show in front of a studio audience, and running into overtime for retakes became expensive (and even their overtime was limited). So even though they did have the chance to correct the mistakes made during the run-through, sometimes even that wasn't enough.

They used the opportunity for retakes from the very first show, when Michael Palin and John Cleese had to redo the sketch in which they spoke gibberish French while describing a diagram of a flying sheep. Even in the version used in the completed show, one can detect the pair close to breaking each other up in midsketch.

In fact, the group was generally quite good about learning their lines (even Johann Gambolputty . . .); their problem was that each of them often tried to make the others laugh while performing—and with quite a degree of success.

One of the best-known cases occurred during the TV series, when Graham Chapman and John Cleese found themselves laughing and unable to stop when they were dressed as older ladies trying to perform the Penguin on the Telly Sketch in the studio. Citing their "complete lack of responsibility," Chapman says they took no notice of the screaming producer, which made it all worse. They eventually completed the scene after about fourteen takes, and they can still be seen stifling laughter in the version that is seen on the TV show.

Michael Palin says that he finds it extremely easy to set off John Cleese, so much so that there is no challenge in it anymore. "I just need to raise an eyebrow, and he's off," Palin boasts.

This was very much in evidence while performing at the Hollywood Bowl. When the pair performed the Dead Parrot Sketch each night, Palin never failed to set off Cleese.

Live shows are fertile ground for similar behavior. Graham Chapman recalled that the group was never able to perform the Police Sketch from start to finish because at least one of them would always start breaking up at one of the others. Props were also a problem in the stage shows, as when Eric Idle's mustache fell off during "Nudge, Nudge"; he simply ad-libbed, "A nod's as good as a wink to a blind mustache."

There were also problems in the various films, although the high cost of moviemaking forced the Pythons to become a bit more serious. The same expenses also caused a few more technical errors to slip through, such as an electrical cable that is in view at the top of the frame during the manger scene in *Life of Brian*.

There were even inconsistencies during the writing process. The spelling of Arthur Putey's name varied from sketch to sketch (Pewtey, Pudey), and Superintendent Harry "Snapper" Organs changed his division as well as his actor (he was played by both Terry Jones and Michael Palin). And during the Sir George Head Mountaineering Sketch, Eric Idle's character, Arthur Wilson, is listed in the stage directions as Bob.

Only a few inconsistencies slipped through in the TV series; five of them are listed below.

1. During the Vocational Guidance Counselor Sketch, John Cleese (in the title role) stumbles over his line and corrects himself: ". . . If I now call Mr. Chipperfield and say to *her* . . .uh, him . . ."
2. On "Interesting People," the man who is half-an-inch long is introduced as Howard Stools, but at the end of his segment, the Compere calls him Alan Stools.
3. The woman told by her milkman that she needs psychiatric treatment is called Mrs. Ratbag, but when she arrives at the psychiatrist's office a few minutes later, her name is Mrs. Pim.
4. Michael Palin, as Police Constable Pan-Am, begins laughing in the middle of his testimony at the trial of Erik Njorl.
5. During the What the Stars Foretell Thesaurus Sketch, the name of Graham Chapman's character changes from Mrs. Trepidatious to Mrs. Ikon in the middle of the sketch.

ythons in Hollywood

Since Monty Python has gone the way of all parrots, the individual members of the group have gone on to a variety of their own projects. In the process, they have also directed and/or co-starred with some of the biggest names in entertainment. The challenge here is to match the stars with the Python member(s) who has worked with them (*NOTE:* Remember, a number of individual projects have involved more than one of the Pythons).

1.	John Belushi	a.	Graham Chapman
2.	Cheech and Chong	b.	John Cleese
3.	Sean Connery	c.	Terry Gilliam
4.	Kevin Costner	d.	Eric Idle
5.	Tim Curry	e.	Terry Jones
6.	Robert De Niro	f.	Michael Palin
7.	Bob Hoskins		
8.	Trevor Howard		
9.	Eartha Kitt		

10. Kevin Kline
11. Andrea Martin
12. Catherine Oxenberg
13. Vanessa Redgrave
14. Mickey Rooney
15. Maggie Smith
16. Robin Williams

Monty Python's Missing Bits

Most of the material the Pythons wrote for the *Flying Circus* ended up in the TV shows, but there were exceptions. When episodes ran several minutes long, sketches were cut and inserted in other shows; but when the shows were only slightly long, brief portions (usually no more than a page or two of script) were cut from shows. In other cases, portions of sketches (or entire sketches themselves) were removed when the shows were distributed in America.

Of course, there were obvious cases of censorship by the BBC, by American television (particularly the 1976 case in which the six shows of the fourth series were severely edited by ABC TV), and even by individual group members themselves. There were even a few instances in which censorship might have been expected but didn't occur (such as the famous Undertakers Sketch).

The TV scripts include parts of sketches that were never filmed as well as some that were completely shot and edited. There are even two complete fifty-minute shows—the famed German specials—that were broadcast only in Germany in the early 1970s; only a few sketches from those have ever been seen by Python fans.

The Python films are another matter. As with most movies, the scripts were revised and edited a great deal, as was the final product. The group published the scripts of *Monty Python and the Holy Grail* and *Life of Brian,* complete with several sections that did not make the final cut; although the complete script for *Meaning of Life* was not published, it also went through a great many revisions, with numerous sections thrown out during the writing process alone.

Fortunately, much of the better material excised from the films (and TV shows) has been recycled in some form or another by the ecological Pythons and has not necessarily been "lost."

Still, considering the quantity of material the six of them produced, there is surprisingly little that was excised from the TV shows and could truly be considered missing. Most of it is listed below, along with some that were significantly different from the versions that ended up in the final shows.

1. "The Wacky Queen"—This was a slapstick bit filmed early in the first series for the "Sex and Violence" show. It was intended to precede the Working-Class Playwright Sketch—in fact, "Playwright" opens with a photograph on the mantel showing the closing shot of "Wacky Queen"—the group had intended for the film segment to lead into "Playwright."

As filmed, "The Wacky Queen" was a Victorian silent film with the voice-over supposedly done by Alfred Lord Tennyson. It opens with Gladstone (Graham Chapman) and Queen Victoria (Terry Jones) walking along the lawn at Osborne. The Queen pushes the gardener into a manure-filled wheelbarrow and then squirts Gladstone with a hose. The tit-for-tat slapstick then builds to a cake-throwing climax.

Alas, the sketch has been clipped from the version of the show released in America (it cuts directly from "Marriage Guidance Counselor" to "Playwright"). Incidentally, the Pythons themselves are not always aware of these changes—Terry Jones, for example, was surprised to hear that the sketch was removed from the show.

2. "Pepperpots on Philosophy"—This was just a bit of additional dialogue cut from the Pepperpots' discussion of French and German philosophers (also from the "Sex and Violence" show).

3. "The Amazing Kargol and Janet"—This brief bit originally appeared in "The Mouse Problem"; Graham Chapman portrayed the first half of this psychiatric conjuring act, which served mostly as a link. Filmed but edited out of the show, it may have served as the predecessor to "The Amazing Mystico and Janet" in the third series, in which Terry Jones erected buildings by hypnosis.

4. "The Italian Lesson Fight"—The classroom sketch in which the teacher (Terry Jones) attempts to teach Italian to a classroom full of native Italians originally ran significantly longer and included a sequence in which a fight breaks out within the class over which city is better, Milan or Naples.

5. "Sandy Camp Arrest"—According to Eric Idle, the BBC cut the final line from the sketch in which a policeman plants a suspicious paper bag on actor Sandy Camp and tries to arrest him. The present version ends with the policeman (Graham Chapman) saying, "Sandwiches? Blimey. Whatever did I give the wife?" The original ending had a shot of the smiling wife saying, "I don't know, but it was better than lunch!," but the BBC wouldn't have it.

6. "The Barber"—One version of this famous sketch ended with the entire tape recording being played through the end of the haircut without the customer wising up, before it was linked to "The Lumberjack Song."

7. "The Visitors"—One early version of this was significantly different from the version that finally aired. The version seen in the show features a young couple who are interrupted from their timid lovemaking by a series of stranger and stranger visitors. The alternate version involves a couple that arrives seven hours late for dinner, and the pajama-clad host, who has gotten out of bed to answer the door, tries to act as though nothing is wrong and remains very polite and British.

This is one alternate version that can stand on its own and is nearly as funny as the very different version used for the TV show.

8. "Arthur Figgis"—The Johann Gambolputty Sketch is preceded by a short bit in which Arthur Figgis signs an autograph that turns into animation. Another sketch was originally intended to precede "Gambolputty"; this one featured three men in a pub trying to recognize another very ordinary, nerdy-looking man (Terry Jones). They make guesses like Jimmy Stewart, Eddie

Waring, and Anthony Newley, but he turns out to be accountant Arthur Figgis.

9. "Buying a Bed"—The original version ran on a great deal longer. The sketch involves people having to say "dog kennel" instead of "mattress" but the original involved a great many other word substitutions, such as "pesos" for "lettuce," before being edited for length.

10. "Interesting People"—As originally written, the Colonel was to have presented this as a sketch that he had written. Cut from it was a segment on Herbert Arkwright, who eats herds of buffalo.

11. "Henry Pratt"—This never-used sketch was to have appeared on the same show as the Jimmy Buzzard interview. It involved a punch-drunk interviewer talking with Pratt, a new British light-heavyweight prospect, who combines a lack of ability with extreme cowardice.

12. "A. t. Hun"—One page was cut from the final version, in which the policeman solves crimes sent in by viewers.

13. "Chelsea Football Team"—The second series was supposed to "kick off" with footballers kicking a ball downfield past John Cleese seated at his desk, with an ending in their changing room. Apparently, Eric Idle was unable to get the team for such a sequence, which the other Pythons didn't let him forget.

14. "Praline and Brookie"—Just before the five animated men pass below the floorboards at their feet, the two characters (played by Cleese and Idle) are in the midst of a chat show (on the "Grillomat" show). Several pages were actually cut from the final version, in which the pair discussed telephone service, with Brookie interjecting homely Yorkshire aphorisms.

15. "1958 Cup Final"—Also on the "Grillomat" show, there was originally a sequence following the Butcher Shop Sketch featuring the 1958 Cup Final discussing the implications of the previous sketch on a chat show.

16. "The Black Spot"—This is probably the best-known example of censorship directed at Terry Gilliam's animation. In the original "Prince and the Black Spot" cartoon, the Prince ignores the spot on his face and dies of cancer. Whenever the show has been repeated, however, another voice has crudely, inexplicably dubbed the word *gangrene* in its place. The version shown in the feature *And Now for Something Completely Different* retains the original *cancer*.

17. "Scott of the Antarctic"—Several sequences were cut from

the final version of the show, including a lunchtime interview with producer Gerry Schlick (Erik Idle), in which he discusses making Evans a girl, and with Terence Lemming (Terry Jones), in which he discusses his character in the film. Another scene was cut in which Bowers fights a dreaded Congolese ringing tarantula (which more-than-slightly resembles a telephone).

18. "Eric the Half-a-Bee"—This is a song meant to accompany the Fish License Sketch; it is, however, included on *Monty Python's Previous Record*.

19. "Football Match"—The match between the Bournemouth Gynecologists and the Watford Long John Silver Impersonators originally had the Watford team face off against the Bournemouth Automobile Association.

20. "Crackpot Religions"—This originally included the Arthur Crackpot Handbook, with such entries as "Blessed are the wealthy, for they have the earth."

21. "Njorl's Saga"—The show was originally going to end with Njorl throwing a pie in his horse's face.

22. "Money Song"—A different song is listed in the script for "The Money Programme," one with more repetitive lyrics.

23. "Summarize Proust"—When Graham Chapman plays Harry Bagot in the "All-England Summarize Proust Competition," he lists his hobbies as "strangling animals, golf, and masturbation." The BBC, however, wiped the word *masturbation* from the audio track, mystifying viewers who hear the subsequent punch line.

24. "Gumby Brain Surgeon"—The original sketch ended with Dr. Gumby pounding on his stomach with a mallet shouting, "Get better, brain!," rather than the surgeon getting into his Gumby uniform.

25. "Lenin's Chartbusters, Volume III"—An animated ad was cut from the final version of the "Cycling Tour" show, with Gilliam's animation selling "twenty-six solid gold tracks" by Lenin.

26. "Big-Nosed Sculptor"—This rather lengthy sketch was intended for the "E. Henry Thripshaw" show late in the third series, as were several other sketches that never appeared on the TV shows, including an early extended version of "Eric the Half-a-Bee."

27. "Cocktails"—This was performed in the early stage shows and can be heard in a slightly different form on the *Live at Drury Lane* album (also intended for the "E. Henry Thripshaw" show).

28. "The Wee-Wee Sketch"—This is probably the most famous Python sketch that never aired; it caused the most dissent within the group. John Cleese apparently tipped off the BBC censor about it because he felt it was a bit childish (although some of the others charged that John couldn't bear anything that had to do with toilet training); there may be some truth to the rumor that it was written solely to annoy Cleese.

The sketch involved a man taking an expert through his wine cellar; the expert would sample different varieties of wine and try to identify them, and the owner would tell him, "No, it's wee-wee."

This is another sketch that even the Pythons were unclear about. Graham Chapman thought it ended up in one of the shows, but even though it was filmed, it never turned up on the TV series.

29. "Politician's Dance"—The "Book at Bedtime" show late in the third series originally began with a party political broadcast in which the speaker (played by John Cleese) ended up dancing with other men in a kick line, followed by animated versions of Wilson and Heath dancing as well. None of the sequence is seen in the version distributed in the United States. Instead, the show begins with a caption saying that the show will start immediately with the opening titles; the original beginning is missing.

30. "The Golden Age of Ballooning"—Cut was a scene at the "Royal Institute for Less-Talented Younger Brothers," with Harpo Nietzsche; the same show also originally included an animated sequence showing America becoming New Scotland.

31. "Michael Ellis"—Much of the material cut from *Monty Python and the Holy Grail* ended up in this show in the fourth series (and is reprinted in its original form in the *Grail* book). Also cut from this show was a scene at the Paisley Counter and one involving an Icelandic honey salesman.

32. "Protest Song"—Neil Innes was originally supposed to perform his "Protest Song" at the end of the "Mr. Neutron" show (the song was a favorite part of the Python stage shows).

33. "The Commanches"—A roller caption linking the Icelandic Honey Sketch and the doctor whose patients are stabbed by his nurse (in the final show of the fourth series), involving Conchito and the Comanche Indian War of 1863, was cut from the show.

34. "Ursula Hitler"—The final show of the fourth series ended

with a look at Ursula Hitler, a Surrey housewife who revolutionized British beekeeping in the 1930s; in 1939, a Mr. Chamberlain sent her an ultimatum on Poland. It followed the closing credits and was apparently removed from the version of the show distributed in America.

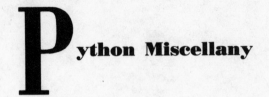

Python Miscellany

LOOKING IT UP

In Britain, the word *Pythonesque* has become a part of everyday language, and it is even listed in some dictionaries.

THE ORIGINAL PYTHON

The remains of a large extinct python were discovered not long ago at the Riversleigh site in Queensland, Australia. Its scientific name is *Montypythonoidesriversleighensis*.

Confuse-a-Cat, Ltd., Recruitment Test

Answers

Not included in the Confuse-a-Cat, Ltd., program are the sixteen-ton weight, Mr. Gumby, and Julius Caesar.

Answers to the First Series: Who Played Who?

1. Terry Jones	11. Terry Jones
2. Eric Idle	12. John Cleese
3. Michael Palin	13. Michael Palin
4. John Cleese	14. Graham Chapman
5. Graham Chapman	15. John Cleese
6. Michael Palin	16. Eric Idle
7. Terry Jones	17. John Cleese
8. Eric Idle	18. Carol Cleveland
9. John Cleese	19. Graham Chapman
10. Graham Chapman	20. Terry Jones

21. Eric Idle	28. Graham Chapman
22. Terry Jones	29. Graham Chapman
23. John Cleese	30. Michael Palin
24. Terry Jones	31. Michael Palin
25. Eric Idle	32. Eric Idle
26. Terry Jones	33. Michael Palin
27. Michael Palin	34. Graham Chapman

Answers to the Second Series: Who Played Who?

1. Terry Jones	17. Eric Idle
2. Michael Palin	18. Terry Jones
3. John Cleese	19. John Cleese
4. Terry Jones	20. Terry Jones
5. Graham Chapman	21. Graham Chapman
6. Eric Idle	22. John Cleese
7. Carol Cleveland	23. Terry Jones
8. Michael Palin	24. Graham Chapman
9. Terry Jones	25. Eric Idle
10. John Cleese	26. Terry Jones
11. Graham Chapman	27. Terry Gilliam
12. Michael Palin	28. Michael Palin
13. Terry Jones	29. Terry Gilliam
14. Terry Gilliam	30. Terry Jones
15. Terry Jones	31. Eric Idle
16. Terry Jones	32. Terry Jones

Answers to the Third Series: Who Played Who?

1. Michael Palin
2. Graham Chapman
3. Eric Idle
4. John Cleese
5. Michael Palin
6. Eric Idle
7. Terry Jones
8. Graham Chapman
9. Terry Jones
10. John Cleese
11. Eric Idle
12. Michael Palin
13. Graham Chapman
14. John Cleese
15. Terry Gilliam
16. Michael Palin
17. Terry Jones
18. Terry Jones
19. Graham Chapman
20. John Cleese
21. Terry Jones
22. Michael Palin
23. John Cleese
24. Eric Idle
25. Michael Palin
26. Michael Palin
27. Graham Chapman
28. John Cleese
29. Michael Palin
30. Eric Idle

Answers to the Fourth Series: Who Played Who?

1. Eric Idle
2. Eric Idle
3. Terry Jones
4. Michael Palin
5. Terry Gilliam
6. Graham Chapman
7. Eric Idle
8. Graham Chapman
9. Terry Jones
10. Eric Idle
11. Graham Chapman
12. Eric Idle
13. Graham Chapman
14. Terry Gilliam
15. Michael Palin
16. Terry Gilliam
17. Michael Palin (and the rest of the group in the "Hamlet" show)

175

Answers to the Dead Parrot War

Mr. Praline: Definitely deceased, bleeding demised, not pining, passed on, is no more, ceased to be, expired, meet its maker, stiff, bereft of life, rests in peace, pushing up the daisies, rung down the curtain, joined the choir invisible, ex-parrot.

Shopkeeper: Resting, stunned, tired and shagged out, pining (for the fiords), kipping (on its back).

Answers to Olympic Hide-and-Seek—Finding Don Roberts

1. b
2. c
3. d
4. a
5. a

BONUS: Huron was found in a sweetshop in Kilmarnock

John Cleese's Favorite Insults—The Answers

1. c
2. b
3. e
4. g
5. a
6. h
7. f
8. d

Answers to Look Who's Talking

1. "Archaeology Today"
2. "Election Night Special"
3. "Party Political Broadcast"
4. "Timmy Williams' Coffee Time"
5. "The Epilogue"

176

6. "It's a Tree"
7. "The Toad Elevating Moment"
8. "The Money Programme"
9. "Party Hints by Veronica"
10. "Blood, Devastation, Death, War, and Horror"
11. "Probe"
12. "Is There?"
13. "Party Political Broadcast"
14. "Grandstand"
15. "The Great Debate"
16. "Thrust"
17. "It's"
18. "The Bols Story"
19. "World Forum"
20. "Farming Club"
21. "How to Do It"
22. "Face the Press"
23. "It's the Arts"
24. "Spectrum"
25. "It's the Arts"

Answers to Mostly Easy Questions: The First Series

1. Only one perfectly ordinary garden shed (A few years ago, he said he was thinking of getting another one)
2. A dead crab
3. Sheep
4. A dirty fork (Lucky he didn't say anything about the dirty knife!)
5. Fresh fruit
6. Confuse-a-Cat, Ltd.
7. A burglar
8. Crunchy frog (If they took the bones out, it wouldn't be crunchy)
9. Giant blancmanges from the planet Skyron in the galaxy of Andromeda
10. Scotland
11. A mattress (Mr. Lambert puts a paper bag over his head when he hears the word *mattress*)

12. A parrot (apparently dead)
13. The Hell's Grannies
14. The Llama
15. A lumberjack!
16. Chartered accountancy
17. Across the English Channel
18. Pearl Harbor
19. The Upper-Class Twit of the Year
20. A group of squatters
21. An albatross!

Answers to Mostly Easy Questions: The Second Series

1. Doug and Dinsdale Piranha
2. The Ministry of Silly Walks
3. Fear, surprise, a ruthless efficiency, and an almost fanatical devotion to the Pope (Oops!)
4. Deja vu
5. Masonry
6. "Blackmail"
7. Ken Clean-Air Systems
8. *2001: A Space Odyssey*
9. Throatwobbler Mangrove
10. The Silly party
11. Parrots
12. Attila the Bun
13. What is the main food that penguins eat?
14. Ratcatching; he runs the Rodent Exterminating Boutique
15. A Sniveling Little Rat-Faced Git
16. Bruce
17. On top of the television set (on the telly!)
18. "Scott of the Sahara"
19. Eric
20. Crackpot Religions, Ltd. (as President and God)
21. Lenin, Karl Marx, Mao Tse-tung, and Che Guevara
22. Spam (Spam, Spam, Spam . . .)
23. Each other

Answers to Mostly Easy Questions: The Third Series

1. Iceland
2. Jean-Paul Sartre
3. Tchaikovsky
4. Brian Norris
5. The room for an argument
6. The Pantomime Horse
7. Marcel Proust
8. Mt. Everest
9. Mr. Smoke-Too-Much
10. The brontosaurus
11. Mollusks (and their sex lives)
12. Biggles
13. None at all—this question is a deliberate waste of time.
14. His hands are severed by the piano lid.
15. Mr. Pither (as in brotherhood, except with "Pi" instead of the "bro," and no "hood"
16. Mr. Gulliver
17. Hide-and-Seek (second leg)
18. The Amazing Mystico
19. Tudor Pornography
20. Dr. E. Henry Thripshaw's Disease, of course
21. Dennis Moore
22. Concorde
23. No time to lose
24. Urine

Answers to Mostly Easy Questions: The Fourth Series

1. The Montgolfier brothers
2. An ant
3. Michael Ellis
4. "Show jumping from White City" (the horses jump over the casts)
5. Cole Porter
6. A private dick
7. The champ's head

8. Teddy Salad
9. "The Most Awful Family in Britain"

Tips for Self-Defense Answers

1. b
2. d
3. c
4. a

Answers to Titles and Topics: The Python Documentary Quiz

1. h
2. o
3. k
4. c
5. d
6. p
7. f
8. m
9. j
10. g
11. i
12. l
13. b
14. e
15. a
16. n

Answers to the Nobody Expects the Spanish Inquisition Quiz

1. Nobody
2. Fear, surprise, ruthless efficiency, an almost fanatical devotion to the Pope, and nice red uniforms
3. The rack, the soft cushions, and the comfy chair
4. She is tied to the rack.

5. She is poked with the soft cushions, and made to sit in the comfy chair until lunchtime, with only a cup of tea at eleven
6. Heresy by thought, heresy by word, heresy by deed, and heresy by action
7. Cardinal Biggles and Cardinal Fang

Answers to the Whizzo Chocolate Quiz

The Whizzo Quality Assortment contains Cherry Fondue, Crunchy Frog, Ram's Bladder Cup, Cockroach Cluster, Anthrax Ripple, and Spring Surprise.

Answers to The *Monty Python and the Holy Grail* Quiz

1. Swedish
2. Terry Gilliam
3. An African swallow, but they are nonmigratory
4. Ninepence
5. King Arthur
6. Because they're made of wood
7. Sir Bedevere
8. A cow
9. He runs away
10. The Castle Anthrax
11. It
12. A shrubbery
13. Tim the Enchanter, Sir Robin
14. He is killed by the deadly rabbit.
15. The Bridge of Death

Answers to the First Series: Lines

1. Arthur Frampton
2. Luigi Vercotti
3. Arthur Putey
4. The Barber
5. Sir Edward Ross
6. Camel Spotter
7. Jimmy Buzzard
8. Inspector Tiger
9. Alexander the Great
10. Mr. Thomas Walters
11. Rt. Hon. Lambert Warbeck
12. Mozart
13. The Colonel
14. Sir George Head
15. Hopkins
16. Mr. Praline
17. Police Constable Henry Thatcher
18. Arthur Lemming
19. Mr. Anchovy
20. David Unction
21. Ken Shabby
22. Irving C. Saltzberg
23. Ken Biggles

Answers to the Second Series: Lines

1. Mr. Engelbert Humperdinck
2. L. F. Dibley
3. A Sniveling Little Rat-Faced Git
4. Chris Conger
5. The Butler
6. Air Chief Marshal Sir Vincent "Kill the Japs" Forster
7. Mr. Anemone
8. The Milkman
9. Mr. Wiggin (of Ironside & Malone)
10. Neville Shunt
11. Archbishop Nudge
12. Gavin Millarrrrrrrrr
13. Arthur Crackpot
14. Timmy Williams
15. Raymond Luxury-Yacht
16. Hank Spim
17. Vanilla Hoare
18. Eric Praline
19. Cardinal Ximinez
20. Ewan McTeagle
21. BBC Man
22. Attila the Hun
23. M. Brando
24. Bruces
25. Karl Marx
26. Hungarian
27. Padre
28. Mr. Ohn Ith
29. Reg
30. Thompson

Answers to the Third Series: Lines

1. Biggles
2. Dr. E. Henry Thripshaw
3. Mr. Gulliver
4. Mr. Smoke-Too-Much
5. Anne Elk
6. Oscar Wilde
7. The Dirty Vicar
8. Michael Norman Randall
9. Col. Sir John "Teasy-Weasy" Butler
10. Eamonn
11. Queen Erizabeth
12. Beulagh Premise
13. Inspector Gaskell/Sir Philip Sidney
14. Henry Wensleydale
15. Gumby Brain Specialist
16. Sir Jane Russell
17. Mrs. Pither
18. Dennis Moore
19. Merchant Banker
20. Inspector Flying Fox of the Yard
21. Akwekwe
22. Mrs. Shazam
23. Brian Norris
24. Hamrag Yatlerot
25. Mr. Atkinson
26. Clement Onan
27. Rev. Arthur Belling
28. Dr. Lewis Hoad

Answers to the Fourth Series: Lines

1. Mr. Gabriello
2. Mr. Neutron
3. Louis XIV
4. Mrs. Mock Tudor
5. Mrs. Entrail
6. Mrs. Scum
7. Chris Quinn's mother
8. Jacques Montgolfier
9. Squadron Leader
10. Kevin Garibaldi
11. Hamlet
12. Mansfield
13. George III
14. Ferdinand von Zeppelin
15. Percy Shelley

Answers to the Restaurant Sketches Quiz

1. e
2. b
3. d
4. c
5. a
6. g
7. f

Answers to the Arthur and Ken Quiz

1. Ken Buddha
2. Arthur Name
3. Arthur Tree
4. Ken Biggles
5. Ken Dove
6. Ken Shabby
7. Flight Lieutenant Ken Frankenstein
8. Kenny Lust
9. Arthur Wilson
10. Arthur Figgis
11. Arthur Aldridge
12. Arthur Putey
13. Arthur Frampton
14. Arthur Ewing
15. Ken
16. Arthur Jackson
17. Arthur Waring
18. Arthur Lemming
19. Brigadier Arthur Gormanstrop
20. Ken
21. Ken Clean-Air Systems
22. Rev. Arthur Belling
23. Arthur X (animated)
24. Ken Andrews
25. Arthur Crackpot
26. Arthur Reginald Webster and Norman Arthur Potter
27. Ken Russell
28. Arthur Ludlow

29. Ken Verybigliar
30. Brigadier Arthur Farquar-Smith
31. Professor Ken Rosewall
32. Arthur Mee
33. Arthur Huntingdon
34. Arthur Huddinut
35. Arthur Hotchkiss
36. Ken
37. Inspector Arthur Perry
38. Sir Kenneth Clark
39. Arthur Briggs
40. Ken S.C.U.M.
41. Kenneth Entrail
42. Arthur Lord Tenniscourt

BONUS FILM QUESTIONS: (a) Arthur Jarrett, who also sang "Christmas in Heaven" after he died (b) King Arthur (this is possibly the easiest question in this entire book, so if you missed it, you're probably in very big trouble . . .)

Answers to Pythons and Other Animals: The Quiz

FIRST SERIES

1. h
2. r
3. l, q
4. f
5. a
6. m
7. b, g, p
8. g
9. n
10. i
11. o
12. j
13. k
14. c
15. e
16. d

SECOND SERIES

1. m
2. i
3. a
4. h
5. g
6. j
7. d
8. e
9. b, k
10. c
11. f
12. l

THIRD SERIES

1. j
2. h
3. c
4. g
5. b
6. a
7. k
8. d
9. f, i
10. e

FOURTH SERIES

1. e
2. d
3. b
4. c
5. a

Not-Quite-as-Easy **First Series** Answers

1. Ernest Scribbler
2. Tread on his corns
3. A clever sheep (specifically, Harold)
4. He was a character witness
5. Dynamo Tension!
6. The planet Skyron in the galaxy of Andromeda
7. One penny
8. 800 pounds
9. Bread, milk, tea, a tin of meat for the cat
10. At the Hairdressers Training Centre at Totnes
11. In the soft-toy department
12. Three tins of beans
13. He has a lion tamer's hat
14. Neap's End
15. Luigi Vercotti
16. Sicily
17. His own boutique
18. Shabby's gran raises polecats

Not-Quite-as-Easy **Second Series** Answers

1. La Marche Futile
2. Nobody expects the Spanish Inquisition!
3. He nailed her head to a coffee table
4. A nude man
5. The phenomenon of deja vu
6. Sea Bass
7. The Royal Society for Putting Things on Top of Other Things
8. "Seven Brides for Seven Brothers"
9. Dung
10. Throatwobbler Mangrove
11. Almost negligible
12. Sheep
13. There is *no* rule six
14. St. Loony Up the Cream Bun and Jam
15. Eight o'clock

16. The Gynecologists
17. Eric (he is an halibut)
18. This is a trick question—Coventry City has never won the FA Cup.
19. Not to stand up
20. The Insurance Sketch
21. Mrs. Nesbitt

Not-Quite-as-Easy Third Series Answers

1. Ringo Starr and Lulu
2. North Malden
3. Mrs. Essense
4. Orphans
5. Tony M. Nyphot
6. They burst into laughter at everything he says
7. The girl with the biggest tits
8. It collapses and is replaced by an NCP Carpark
9. The Limpet
10. Campbell's Cream of Mushroom Soup
11. The cat had gotten to it
12. Bolivia (La Paz)
13. He thought it better to consult a man with some professional qualifications.
14. Edward Heath
15. They're all dead
16. Characters from 19th century English literature
17. "Dr. E. Henry Thripshaw's Disease"
18. BBC program planners
19. HRH the Dummy Princess Margaret
20. The cast of the Dirty Vicar Sketch

Not-Quite-as-Easy Fourth Series Answers

1. Jacques
2. The Ronettes
3. It's cheaper to buy a new one than to feed one, so there's a constant variety of companions
4. The sperm whale

5. "When Does a Dream Begin?"
6. Queen Victoria
7. In the Yukon (pulling a dogsled)
8. Mr. Neutron
9. A radio, a telephone, and the cat

Stocking the Cheese Shop Answers

It is, of course, a trick question. *All* of the cheeses listed were requested by the customer, and, of course, none of them were available.

Answers to Python Fun and Game Shows

1. e
2. c
3. g
4. h
5. a
6. k
7. l
8. b
9. m
10. i
11. j
12. d
13. f

Answers to the Poems, Plays, and Porn Quiz

1. b
2. c
3. a
4. c
5. a
6. c
7. a
8. b
9. c
10. a

Answers to Amazing Activities

1. b
2. a
3. c
4. a
5. c
6. a
7. b
8. d
9. a
10. d
11. d
12. c

Answers to Historical Impersonations: The Quiz

1. d
2. c
3. f
4. i
5. e, h
6. g
7. a
8. b

Answers to the Religion, Ltd. Quiz

1. f
2. e
3. b
4. a
5. d
6. g
7. h
8. c

Answers to the Monty Python's *Life of Brian* Quiz

1. The myrrh
2. Stones (two points, two flats, and a packet of gravel)
3. *Jehovah* (as in, "That piece of halibut was good enough for Jehovah")
4. Sixteen years (and proud of it!)
5. The name given by the centurion who fathered Brian
6. Stan (he wants to be called Loretta)
7. The People's Front of Judea
8. He tries to write "Romans, Go Home" (which he misspells as "Romanes Eunt Domus" instead of "Romani, Ite Domum").
9. Pilate's wife
10. The Campaign for a Free Galilee
11. Biggus Dickus
12. A gourd
13. Those who follow the shoe, those who follow the sandal, and those who follow the gourd
14. Eighteen years
15. "Always Look on the Bright Side of Life"

Python Rocks!

1. e
2. a (Paul Simon also did a series of similar interviews.)
3. d
4. f (He was unrecognized as he joined the mountie chorus and sang along to "The Lumberjack Song.")
5. b
6. j
7. f, h (In addition to a similar, equally unrecognized appearance in the Lumberjack chorus, he also performed "The Pirate Song" on Idle's TV show)
8. i (Keith, a close friend of Graham's, died a month before filming was to start.)
9. g (He had a brief cameo role as a cavalry officer.)
10. c

Answers to Fill in the Missing Words: The First Series

1. Vicki Carr
2. False Teeth
3. Eddie-Baby
4. sheep
5. gala luncheons
6. goer
7. murder
8. blancmange impersonator
9. dirty knife
10. Confuse-a-Cat
11. Notlob
12. Name
13. Harrod's
14. one hump
15. twelve feet
16. fish
17. bricks
18. three
19. Stalingrad
20. mattress
21. Cicely Courtneidge
22. Karl Gambolputty de von Ausfern-schplenden-schlitter-crasscrenbon-fried-digger-dingle-dangle-dongle-dungle-burstein-von-knacker-thrasher-apple-banger-horowitz-ticolensic-grander-knotty-spelltinkle-grandlich-grumblemeyer-spelterwasser-kurstlich-himbleeisen-bahnwagen-gutenabend-bitte-ein-nurnburger-bratwustle-gerspurten-mitz-weimache-luber-hundsfut-gumberaber-shonendanker-kalbsfleisch-mittler-aucher von Hautkopft of Ulm

Answers to Fill in the Missing Words: The Second Series

1. Crump-Pinnet
2. weapon
3. Two-Lumps

4. legs
5. grahnd piano
6. slaughter
7. nude lady
8. semprini
9. repetition
10. Silly
11. Dibley
12. Paignton
13. Attila the Hun
14. mosquito
15. mynah bird
16. contradicting
17. polystyrene
18. housing
19. *vomit*
20. Crelm toothpaste
21. twelve
22. bird-watchers' eggs
23. concrete truss
24. tiger's bum
25. lounge suite

Answers to Fill in the Missing Words: The Third Series

1. twenty
2. North Malden
3. dead cat
4. Brian Norris
5. play the flute
6. argument
7. Hamrag Yatlerot
8. Househunters
9. five
10. Everest
11. Marcel Proust
12. Lake Pahoe
13. Ilchester
14. Clodagh Rogers

15. luggage compartment
16. "Paradise Lost"
17. "Gay Boys in Bondage"
18. Amontillado
19. botany lesson
20. penguin
21. "No Time Toulouse"
22. David Niven
23. poetry
24. Clambake
25. brain

Answers to Fill in the Missing Words: The Fourth Series

1. anteater
2. walking
3. claret
4. Zeppelin
5. Marcus
6. wet towels
7. caribou
8. Ballet
9. Most Awful
10. unclogs
11. gaiters
12. *Cutty Sark*

Answers to the History and Literature Quiz

First Series: Edgar Allan Poe, King Arthur, and King Henry the VIII did not appear in the first series. *BONUS:* Julius Caesar and Napoléon each appeared in three separate sketches.

Second Series: Captain Ahab, Catherine the Great, Oliver Twist, and Adolf Hitler did not appear in the second series.

Third Series: All of the characters listed appeared in the third series. *BONUS:* Clodagh Rogers, Trotsky, Eartha Kitt, and Edward Heath were played by Mr. Gulliver in "Cycling Tour"; Princess Margaret was portrayed as a dummy and a pantomime character.

Fourth Series: Cleopatra and Galileo did not appear in the fourth series.

Answers to the Missing Links

1. n
2. c
3. h
4. e
5. l
6. f
7. p
8. g
9. j
10. a
11. i
12. d
13. o
14. m
15. k
16. b

Answers to Brain Hurters: The First Series

1. The policemen of Q Division
2. They go cycling together
3. Squirting Vermeer's *Lady at a Window* with black aerosol
4. Arthur Ewing trained 23 mice to squeak in different pitches
5. Flopsy the Rabbit
6. It's-a-great-idea-but-possibly-not-and-I'm-not-being-indecisive
7. Anyone who saw the crime, ladies with large breasts, or just anyone who likes policemen

8. Forty-eight million kilts
9. On the side of the engine, above the piston box
10. Jimmy Blenkinsop
11. Bolton
12. *Physique*
13. He believes that Drake was too clever for the German fleet
14. Gervaise Brook-Hampster
15. The National Bocialist party
16. frogs
17. Brian London
18. U-P-Y-O-U-R-S

Answers to Brain Hurters: The Second Series

1. Mrs. G. Pinnet
2. The giant hedgehog was 800 yards long
3. A tax on "thingy"
4. Six years
5. A convenient bale of hay
6. Alfred Lord Tennyson
7. He has a steel peg driven into his skull with a mallet, or if he's in a deep sleep, his head is sawed off
8. The man from the off-license
9. Basil
10. Six-foot five
11. Roy Spim
12. "Michelangelo's Fifth Symphony "
13. The Prime Minister
14. A city gent at the beginning of the Fish License Sketch
15. Sir Horace was killed by his son Tony for his train reservation
16. It's over there in a box
17. Alexander Yahlt
18. The Green Midget Café at Bromley
19. September 1713
20. More than 400

Answers to Brain Hurters: The Third Series

1. Betty-Muriel
2. In Mrs. Kelly's boarding room
3. *The Lady with the Naked Skin* by Paul Fox, Jr.
4. A chartered accountant
5. Mr. Akwekwe
6. Panther
7. Room 12A (next door)
8. They find the camera crews filming them
9. The Durham Light Infantry
10. Twelve hours
11. Her cello
12. King Haakon of Norway and Princess Margaret
13. The number four
14. Shirley Bassey
15. They are keen on cricket and bingo
16. Four million pounds
17. *Tits and Bums* and *Shower Sheila*
18. Swag
19. Basil
20. The new Oxford Professor of Fine Arts
21. *Ivanhoe*
22. A severed leg

Answers to Brain Hurters: The Fourth Series

1. Norway has a high per capita income, a fourteen percent industrial reinvestment rate, and girls with massive knockers
2. Because two of its legs are missing
3. Cole Porter
4. Pixie hats with ears
5. His fighter's head
6. Disguise
7. "My Mistake"
8. The nurse

Answers to Animations of Gilliam: The Quiz

FIRST SERIES

1. g
2. d
3. i
4. f
5. b
6. e
7. h
8. a
9. c

SECOND SERIES

1. e
2. h
3. a
4. i
5. c
6. f
7. b
8. g
9. d

THIRD AND FOURTH SERIES

1. e
2. c
3. f
4. g
5. a
6. b
7. h
8. i
9. d

Answers to Onstage, Onscreen, and on the Air

THE FILMS

1. j
2. b
3. f
4. l
5. o
6. k
7. q
8. d
9. p
10. e
11. c
12. n
13. g
14. h
15. a
16. r
17. i
18. b
19. m

THEATER

1. f
2. h
3. j
4. e
5. d
6. g
7. a
8. i
9. k
10. l
11. a
12. k
13. c
14. b

1. i
2. m
3. j
4. b
5. l
6. e
7. o
8. d
9. f
10. n
11. c
12. k
13. a
14. h
15. g

Answers to the Monty Python's Meaning of Life Quiz

1. Just in case the administrator comes
2. Sell them all for medical experiments
3. Being able to wear a rubber sheath over your old fellow
4. He is preoccupied with an ocarina
5. Several timepieces, including a grandfather's clock and a wristwatch as well as a birthday cake and a check
6. A tiger (or possibly men in a tiger costume) steals it
7. Terry Gilliam in drag (wearing a Little Bo Peep–like costume)
8. Philosophy (specifically the meaning of life), although they do get sidetracked
9. A liver
10. People aren't wearing enough hats, and matter is energy
11. He explodes after eating a wafer-thin mint
12. He is chased off a cliff by a mob of beautiful, seminude women with cricket bats
13. The salmon mousse (made with canned salmon)
14. The couples each drive there
15. "Christmas in Heaven"

Answers to Pythons in Hollywood

1. d, f (in *All You Need Is Cash* and *Saturday Night Live)*
2. a, b, d (in *Yellowbeard)*
3. c, b, f (in *Time Bandits)*
4. b (in *Silverado)*
5. f (in a TV production of *Three Men in a Boat)*
6. c, f (in *Brazil)*
7. c, f (in *Brazil)*; also e (recorded some *Fairy Tales* for a record based on his book)
8. f (in *The Missionary)*
9. e, b (in *Erik the Viking)*
10. b, f (in *A Fish Called Wanda)*; also b (in *Silverado)*
11. d (in *Too Much Sun)*
12. a (in *Still Crazy Like a Fox)*
13. e, f (in *Consuming Passions*, based on their play *Secrets)*
14. e, b (in *Erik the Viking)*
15. f (in both *The Missionary* and *A Private Function)*
16. c, d (in *The Adventures of Baron Munchausen)*; also c (in *The Fisher King)*